COLLINS

MODERN
TANKS

HarperCollins*Publishers*

Text by Chris Foss

Thanks to Mr William Crampton of the FI for the flags
Front cover: Frank Spooner Pictures

HarperCollins*Publishers*
PO Box, Glasgow G4 0NB

First Published 1995
© HarperCollins*Publishers* 1995

Flags © The Flag Institute 1995

ISBN 0 00 4708482

Printed in Italy by Amadeus S.p.A.,Rome

CONTENTS

| 6 | Introduction: Tank development 1945-95 | |

Main Battle Tanks

20	SK 105	Austria
22	Type 85	China
24	Type 80	China
26	Type 69	China
28	Type 63	China
30	Leclerc	France
32	AMX-30B2	France
34	AMX-13	France
36	Leopard 2	Germany
38	Leopard 1	Germany
40	TAM	Germany
42	Merkava	Israel
44	Ariete	Italy
46	OF-40	Italy
48	Type 90	Japan
50	Type 74	Japan
52	Type 61	Japan
54	T-80U	Russia
56	T-72S	Russia
58	T-64B	Russia
60	T-62	Russia
62	T-54	Russia
64	T-34	Russia
66	PT-76	Russia
68	Type 88	South Korea
70	S-tank	Sweden
72	Ikv-91	Sweden
74	Pz 68	Switzerland
76	Challenger 2	UK
78	Challenger 1	UK
80	Chieftain	UK
82	Centurion	UK
84	Vickers Mk3	UK
86	Scorpion	UK
88	M1 Abrams	USA
90	M60	USA
92	M48	USA
94	M47	USA
96	M4A3	USA
98	XM8	USA
100	Stingray	USA
102	M551	USA
104	M41	USA
106	M84	Yugoslavia

CONTENTS

Armoured cars

108	EE-9	Brazil
110	EE-3	Brazil
112	AMX-10RC	France
114	ERC	France
116	AML90	France
118	VBL	France
120	Luchs	Germany
124	FUG	Hungary
126	RAM	Israel
128	Centauro	Italy
130	Type 6616	Italy
132	Type 87	Japan
134	Type 82	Japan
136	BRDM-2	Russia
138	BRDM-1	Russia
140	Rooikat	South Africa
142	VEC	South Africa
144	Saladin	UK
146	Shortland	UK
148	Ferret	UK
150	Scout	USA
152	M8	USA

Armoured personnel carriers

154	4K 7FA	Austria
156	Pandur	Austria
158	Sibmas	Belgium
160	EE-11	Brazil
162	BMP-30	Bulgaria
164	Y531	China
166	Y531C	China
168	OT-64	Czech Republic
170	Fahd	Egypt
172	AMX-10P	France
174	VCI	France
176	VAB	France
178	VCR	France
180	M3	France
182	Marder	Germany
184	Fuchs	Germany
186	Condor	Germany
188	TM170	Germany
190	PSZH	Hungary
192	Type 6614	Italy
194	Type 73	Japan

CONTENTS

196	Su-60	Japan	244	AAV7	USA
198	BMP-3	Russia	246	LAV300	USA
200	BMP-2	Russia	248	LAV150	USA
202	BMP-1	Russia	250	Ranger	USA
204	BMD	Russia	252	BVP80	Yugoslavia
206	BTR-80	Russia	254	BOV	Yugoslavia
208	BTR-70	Russia			
210	BTR-60	Russia			
212	MTLB	Russia			
214	Ratel	South Africa			
216	Casspir	South Africa			
218	Mamba	South Africa			
220	BLR	Spain			
222	BMR 600	Spain			
224	CV 9040	Sweden			
226	Pbv 302	Sweden			
228	Piranha	Switzerland			
230	Warrior	UK			
232	FV432	UK			
234	Saxon	UK			
236	Saracen	UK			
238	S55	UK			
240	Bradley	USA			
242	M113	USA			

Introduction: Tank development 1945-95

This pocketbook provides technical information and photographs of 117 of the key Armoured Fighting Vehicles (AFVs) currently in service all over the world. It does not pretend to be a comprehensive work of reference covering every type of AFV that is under development or in service.

This book does not cover supporting armoured vehicles such as self-propelled guns, mobile air defence systems or the host of engineer vehicles without which no modern army could remain effective.

For easy reference, this book is divided into three sections: Main Battle Tanks and Light Tanks, Armoured Cars and Scout Vehicles and Infantry Fighting Vehicles and Armoured Personnel Carriers. Within each section, the latest vehicle is normally given first with the oldest last. For example, under the United Kingdom, the latest MBT, the Vickers Defence Systems Challenger 2 (now entering service with the British Army) is covered first, followed by the Challenger 1, Chieftain, Centurion Mk 13, Vickers Defence Systems Mk 3 and, finally, the Alvis Scorpion light tank.

Each entry includes key specifications, comments on development and unique features, as well as a list of variants and current status. For some vehicles there are simply too many variants to list, so that only the key production variants are listed.

An Oliphant Mk 1B of the South African Defence Force

It should also be remembered that many countries, for example Israel and South Africa, have carried out many local modifications to their vehicles which have resulted in what is virtually a new vehicle bearing little external resemblance to the original imported vehicle. A good example is the British Centurion MBT which was developed towards the end of the Second World War. It was phased out of service with the British Army in the 1960s when it was replaced by the Chieftain. The Centurion is still in front line service with a number of countries with the latest South African Olifant Mk 1B being virtually a new vehicle with new powerpack, suspension, turret systems and armour.

Main Battle Tanks

Until the early 1960s, some armies operated three types of tank: light, medium and heavy. Examples of the latter include the Russian T-10, armed with a 122 mm (4.8 in) gun, and the British Conqueror and US M103, both armed with a 120 mm (4.7 in) gun. These tanks all featured a powerful gun and a very high degree of armour protection, but they lacked mobility. From the 1960s these heavy tanks were phased out of service and most armies then just used one type of tank, often referred to as the Main Battle Tank (MBT). These usually weigh around 40 tonnes (88, 000 lb) and are armed with a 100 mm or 105 mm gun.

The three basic aspects of tank design are armour, mobility and firepower, but each of these can be sub-divided even further. For example, firepower includes not only the calibre of the main armament, but also the armour penetration characteristics of the ammunition, the accuracy of the fire control system and the type of sighting system fitted. Even with the best equipment in the world, unless the crew are motivated and trained to use this, it will be worthless on the battlefield.

Several early MBTs such as the Leopard 1 had excellent firepower and mobility, but lower armour protection. By contrast, the British Chieftain,

The heavily protected Chieftain with its 120mm gun

developed at the same time as the Leopard 1 has excellent armour and firepower but poor mobility. Second generation MBTs such as the US M1 have excellent armour, mobility and firepower. They are much heavier than the first generation MBTs, incorporate all manner of advanced technologies and are far more expensive. For this reason the number of countries that can afford to operate and maintain this type of MBT is limited.

The French call their new Leclerc MBT a third generation MBT because not only does it have good armour, mobility and firepower, but it is also smaller than the Leopard 2 and M1A1 Abrams, with a three man crew due to the introduction of an automatic loader. The latter is not a new feature as Russian tanks, including the T-64, T-72, T-80 and more recent T-90 all have an automatic loader for their 125 mm (4.9 in) smooth bore guns.

Over the last 25 years there have been major advances in tank technology. The latest generation MBTs feature advanced computerised fire control systems and stabilised day/thermal sights that enable targets to be hit with the first round fired at ranges of over 2000 m (2200 yards) by day or night.

For many years MBTs armour was of the cast or

Explosive Reactive Armour panels on a T-72 MBT

Russian T-80s in their new camouflage scheme

welded steel type, but the latest MBTs such as the
Leopard 2, Abrams, Challenger 1 and 2 and the
Leclerc, have new and advanced armours that give a
very high degree of protection against both chemical
energy (CE) and kinetic energy (KE) attack over their
frontal arc.

A number of countries are now installing Explosive
Reactive Armour (ERA) on their MBTs and some of
their lighter armoured vehicles as well, to improve
their battlefield survivability against weapons fitted
with a HEAT (High Explosive Anti-Tank) warhead.
Israel was the first country to fit ERA on MBTs for
combat, during the 1982 invasion of the Lebanon,
and these saved many Centurion and M48/M60
MBTs from loss when they were hit by Russian

supplied AT-3 Sagger anti-tank guided missiles and RPG-7 rocket propelled grenades. Russia had already developed ERA but had not decided to fit it to its tanks. Following the successful introduction of ERA by the Israeli Army, the Russian Army soon started to fit ERA to its tanks which already had a high degree of battlefield survivability. Today virtually all Russian MBT's are fitted with ERA but recent events in Chechnia proved that they were still vulnerable when fighting in a city, unsupported by infantry.

Due to weight and other design considerations, the highest level of protection on the MBT is given only over their frontal arcs as this is considered the most likely area of attack. Over their rear arc, virtually all MBTs are highly vulnerable to anything larger than 12.7 mm (0.50 in) machine gun fire.

Most MBTs are now fitted with day and night vision equipment but for many years the latter has been of the infra-red or image intensification type. Some countries, for example France (Leclerc), Germany (Leopard 2), UK (Challenger 1 and 2) and the US (M1 series) have now fielded MBTs with thermal night vision devices, enabling the MBT to engage targets under virtually all weather conditions.

In the future, MBTs will have advanced defensive aids systems as most combat aircraft do. Indeed, the Russian Army has already started to fit defensive aids

The Merkava's engine is at the front for extra protection

systems to their key MBTs. Their very high cost means that it will be many years, if at all, before all of their MBTs are fitted with these devices.

The future prospects of the tank have been doubted ever since tanks first appeared on the battlefields of the First World War. Some authorities questioned the future of the tank right up to 1940. The development of new anti-tank weapons after the Second World War led to new prophesies that the tank would have no future on modern battlefields. This was especially true after the early setbacks of the Israeli Armoured Corps during the 1973 Middle East conflict. Israeli MBTs operating without infantry, artillery or close air support suffered heavy casualties at the hands of the

Egyptian Army, especially from the man portable AT-3 Sagger anti-tank guided weapon and the RPG-7 rocket-propelled grenade.

Following this conflict the major powers placed increased emphasis on combined arms operations with armour, infantry, artillery, enginer and close air support (both fixed wing and helicopters) all working together.

The Allied Coalition Forces placed great emphasis on combined arms operations during Operation Desert Storm in February 1990 and so inflicted heavy casualties on the Iraqi forces with little loss to themselves. However, it must be stressed that the Iraqi Army had been subjected to a month of aerial bombardment. Although the Iraqi Army had some of the best equipment of any army in the Middle East, it did not come up to the same standard as that of the British and US armies that took part in Desert Storm. Not only did these have much better equipment, but they were far better trained, motivated and led. While the Iraqi Army did have some modern equipment, for example the Russian T-72 MBT, it only had the early model which is clearly inferior to the American M1A1 and the British Challenger 1. One reason why the Challenger 1 and M1A1 did excel is that their thermal night sights gave them the added advantage of being able to engage targets in virtually all weather conditions.

The XM-8 is to replace the US Army's M551 Sheridans

Most MBTs are now fitted with some type of NBC (Nuclear, Biological and Chemical) defence system. MBTs in the future are likely to be smaller and may well have a two man crew. They will also incorporate stealth technology and will have a new type of main armament, possibly an electro-thermal weapon.

Light tanks

After many years in decline, the light tank is now making a comeback, although very often it is not called a light tank at all, for example, the US 105 mm armed XM8 Armored Gun System (AGS) currently under development for the US Army as the replacment for the older M551 Sheridan fielded over

15

25 years ago. In some parts of the world the terrain is such that it is difficult to use MBTs so light tanks, which usually have a lower ground pressure than MBTs, have a number of advantages.

A feature of many of the more recent light tanks is that they can be carried inside the widely deployed Lockheed C-130 Hercules transport aircraft. A good example of this is the new United Defense XM8 Armored Gun System.

Armoured Cars and Scout Cars

These are the eyes and ears of the army units. They do not engage enemy MBTs because they lack the firepower to penetrate their armour. Normally they

The distinctive 8 x 8 Rooikat with its 76 mm gun

A heavily-modified M41 of the Brazilian army

would report the strength and direction of the enemy movement and then try to keep them under observation.

Armament of this type of vehicle ranges from a 7.62 mm machine gun up to a 105 mm rifled tank gun with the turret being fitted with a computerised fire control system. Armoured cars such as the Italian IVECO/OTOBREDA B1, are armed with a 105 mm gun. This type of vehicle has the same firepower as the Leopard 1 MBT, good cross-country mobility and a much wider operational range than a tracked vehicle. The only area in which it is inferior is in armour protection.

17

IFVs and APCs

Today there are two basic types of vehicle used to transport infantry: the infantry fighting vehicle (IFV) and the armoured personnel carrier (APC). The IFV normally has a higher degree of protection than the APC and has good cross country mobility because it has keep up with the MBTs. Sometimes the IFV is fitted with firing ports to allow some of the infantry to use their small arms from within the vehicle in complete safety. The APC is normally used to transport the infantry as close to their objective as possible when they then dismount and fight on foot. A good example of the better armed vehicle is the US Bradley infantry fighting vehicle which is fitted with a two man power operated turret armed with a stabilised 25 mm cannon, 7.62 mm co-axial machine gun and a launcher for the TOW anti-tank guided weapon. The new Russian BMP-3 ICV is even more heavily armed as it is fitted with a two man turret armed with a 100 mm gun that can fire an anti-tank guided missile as well as conventional ammunition. A 30 mm cannon and 7.62 mm machine gun is mounted co-axial with the 100 mm gun and the vehicle also has two bow mounted 7.62 mm machine guns.

While the tracked vehicles have greater cross-country mobility than most of their wheeled counterparts, the latter tend to be cheaper to operate and maintain and

The revolutionary BMP infantry fighting vehicle

have greater strategic mobility. Wheeled APCs have a lower level of armour protection than their tracked counterparts and are therefore more vulnerable on the battlefield. Most APCs have all welded steel or aluminium hulls that provide protection from small arms fire and shell splinters. As a result of operational experience in the Middle East and while operating with the United Nations, a number of countries have provided their vehicles with additional armour packages to improve their battlefield survivability. These are normally of the passive type, although the US Army is adopting an ERA package for its Bradley infantry fighting vehicle.

Steyr-Daimler-Puch SK 105 Light Tank

The SK105 has a 105 mm gun with an automatic loader

The SK 105 was developed for the Austrian Army for a highly mobile 105mm armed tank destroyer and, within the Austrian Army, it is commonly known as the Kurassier. The first prototype was completed in 1969, with first production vehicles following in 1971 and so far over 600 vehicles have been built for the home and export markets.

The chassis of the SK 105 uses automotive components of the Steyr-Daimler-Puch series of full-tracked armoured personnel carriers, with the turret being based on the French turret. Fitted to the AMX-13 light tank, this turret is of the oscillating type, with the 105mm gun fed by a bustle-mounted automatic loader pivoted on the lower part. The automatic loader holds a total of 12 rounds of 105 mm ammunition, with the empty cartridge cases being ejected out of the turret rear.

Standard equipment includes a laser range-finder, an NBC (Nuclear, Biological, Chemical) system, a HEAT (High Explosive Anti-Tank) and night vision equipment. Further development of the SK 105 for the export market has resulted in the SK 105/A1, SK 105/A2 and SK 105/A3.

Variants
Greif Armoured recovery vehicle
Pionier vehicle/engineer vehicle

Specification

Crew: 3
Armament:
Main: 1x105mm gun
Co-axial: 1 x 7.62mm machine gun
Anti-aircraft: 1 x 7.62mm machine gun
Combat weight: 17,700kg (38,940lb)
Power-to-weight ratio: 18.1hp/t
Length with gun: 7.735m (25.4ft)
Hull length: 5.582m (18.3ft);
Width: 2.5m (8.2ft)

Height: 2.529m (8.3ft)
Ground clearance: 0.4m (1.3ft)
Maximum road speed: 70km/h (43.4mph)
Range: 500km (310 miles)
Vertical obstacle: 0.8m (2.6ft)
Trench crossing: 2.41m (7.9ft)
Fording: 1m (3.3ft)
Powerpack: Steyr 7FA 6-cylinder turbo-charged diesel, developing 320hp coupled to ZF 6 HP 600 automatic transmission.

NORINCO Type 85-IIM MBT

Pakistan is now manufacturing the Type 85 under licence

The Type 85-II MBT has been developed by NORINCO (China North Industries Corporation) for the Chinese Army. The Type 85-II and Type 85-IIA are armed with a 105mm rifled tank gun, but the more recent Type 85-IIM is armed with a 125mm smooth bore gun, fed from an automatic loader, which has enabled the crew to be reduced to three: commander, gunner and driver. The 125mm gun is stabilised in elevation and traverse. The computerised fire control system includes a ballistic computer and a laser range-finder. Mounted around the sides and rear of the turret is a wire cage which can be used to stow equipment.

Standard equipment includes an NBC (Nuclear, Biological, Chemical) system, a fire detection and suppression system, night vision equipment for commander, gunner and driver, and the ability to lay smoke screen by injecting diesel fuel into the exhaust outlet.

The Type 85-IIAP is being manufactured under licence in Pakistan, and further development has resulted in the Type 90-II which has a number of improvements including a more powerful engine, where it is called the Khalid.

Specification

Crew: 3
Armament:
Main: 1 x 125mm gun
Co-axial: 1 x 7.62mm machine gun
Anti-aircraft: 1 x 12.7mm machine gun
Combat weight: 41 000kg (90,000lb)
Power-to-weight ratio: 18.5hp/t
Length with gun: 10.28m (33.7ft)
Hull length: 7.30m (23.9ft)

Width: 3.45m (11.3ft)
Height: 2.30m (7.5ft)
Ground clearance: 0.48m (1.6ft)
Maximum road speed: 57.25km/h (36 mph)
Range: 430km (266 miles)
Vertical obstacle: 0.8m (2.62ft)
Trench crossing: 2.70m (8.9ft)
Fording: 1.4m (4.6ft)
Powerpack: V-12 diesel, developing 730hp coupled to manual transmission.

NORINCO Type 80 MBT

The Type 80-II is used only by the Chinese army itself

The NORINCO (China North Industries Corporation) Type 80 MBT was developed from 1978, with the first prototypes being completed in 1985.

In appearance it is similar to the Type 69, but the cast turret is fitted with a NATO standard 105mm rifled tank gun with a fume extractor and thermal sleeve. The chassis is new and has six road wheels, with the upper part of the suspension covered by skirts. The 105mm gun is stabilised in elevation and traverse, and the computerised fire control system includes a ballistic computer and a laser range-finder. Mounted around the sides and rear of the turret is a wire cage which can be used to stow equipment, and which provides some stand-off protection from HEAT (High Explosive Anti-Tank) projectiles.

Standard equipment includes an NBC (Nuclear, Biological, Chemical) system, a fire detection and suppression system, night vision equipment for commander, gunner and driver, as well as the ability to lay smoke screen by injecting diesel fuel into the exhaust outlet. Mounted at the rear of the hull are long range fuel tanks and an unditching beam. With preparation, the Type 80 MBT can ford to a depth of 1.5m. The Type 80-II has minor differences and is offered with a more advanced fire control system.

Specification

Crew: 4
Armament:
Main: 1 x 105mm gun
Co-axial: 1 x 7.62mm machine gun
Anti-aircraft: 1 x 12.7mm machine gun
Combat weight: 38,000kg (83,600lb)
Power-to-weight ratio: 19.20hp/t
Length with gun: 9.328m (30.6ft)

Hull length: 6.325m (10.9ft)
Width: 3.354m (11ft)
Height: 2.874m (9.6ft)
Ground clearance: 0.48m (1.6ft)
Maximum road speed: 60km/h (37.2mph)
Range: 430km (266.6 miles)
Vertical obstacle: 0.8m (2.6ft)
Trench crossing: 2.70m (8.9ft)
Fording: 1.4m (4.6ft)
Powerpack: V-12 diesel, developing 730hp coupled to manual transmission.

NORINCO Type 69 MBT

Iraq used large numbers of Type 69s in the Gulf War

The Type 69 MBT was first seen in public in 1982, as a further development of the Type 59 MBT, itself a copy of the Russian T-54 MBT. Marketing of the Type 69 MBT is carried out by NORINCO (China North Industries Corporation).

First production of Type 69-I MBTs had a 100mm smooth bore gun, but this was soon followed by the Type 69-II MBT which had a number of improvements including a 100mm rifled tank gun – stabilised in both elevation and traverse – and the installation of a computerised fire control system which also included a laser range-finder for improved first round hit probability.

Standard equipment includes an NBC (Nuclear,

Biological, Chemical) system, a fire detection and suppression system, night vision equipment for commander, gunner and driver, and the ability to lay smoke screen by injecting diesel fuel into the exhaust on the left side of the hull. Local production of the Type 69-II MBT has been undertaken in Pakistan.

Variants
Twin 37mm self-propelled anti-aircraft gun
Twin 57mm Type 80 self-propelled anti-aircraft gun
Type 84 Armoured vehicle-launched bridge
Type 653 Armoured recovery vehicle

Specification

Crew: 4
Armament:
Main: 1 x 100mm gun
Bow: 1 x 7.62mm machine gun
Co-axial: 1 x 7.62mm machine gun
Anti-aircraft: 1 x 12.7mm machine gun
Combat weight: 37,000kg (84,400lb)
Power-to-weight ratio: 15.89hp/t
Length with gun: 8.657m (28.4ft)
Hull length: 6.243m (20.5ft)

Width: 3.298m (10.8ft)
Height: 2.807m (9.21ft)
Ground clearance: 0.425m (4.6ft)
Maximum road speed: 50km/h (31mph)
Range: 430km (267 miles)
Vertical obstacle: 0.8m (2.6ft)
Trench crossing: 2.70m (8.9ft)
Fording: 1.4m (4.6ft)
Powerpack: Type 12150L-7BW V-12 diesel, developing 580hp coupled to manual transmission.

NORINCO 63 Light Tank

North Vietnamese forces used Type 63s in the 1972 offensive and the final conquest of South Vietnam

As part of its military assistance programme, Russia supplied China with a quantity of PT-76 light amphibious tanks in the late 1950s. These were probably manufactured in China under the designation of the Type 60. Futher development in China resulted in the Type 63 light amphibious tank which is very similar in appearance to the Russian PT-76, but which has a different turret of cast sections welded together, is armed with an 85mm gun and has a more powerful engine.

As far as is known, the Type 63 is not fitted with an NBC (Nuclear, Biological, Chemical) system or any type of night vision equipment. As originally built, it was not fitted with a fire control system, although in recent years some vehicles have been observed with a laser range-finder mounted above the mantlet of the 85mm gun to improve the first round hit probability. The Type 63 is fully amphibious, propelled in the water by two water-jets mounted at the rear of the hull. Before entering the water the trim vane is erected at the front of the hull and the bilge pumps switched on.

Specification

Crew: 4
Armament:
Main: 1 x 85mm gun
Co-axial: 1 x 7.62mm machine gun;
Anti-aircraft: 1 x 12.7mm machine gun
Combat weight: 18,700kg (41,140lb)
Power-to-weight ratio: 21.39hp/t
Length with gun: 8.437m (27.7ft)
Hull length: 7.15m (23.4ft)

Width: 3.2m (10.5ft)
Height: 2.522m (8.3ft)
Ground clearance: 0.4m (1.4ft)
Maximum road speed: 64km/h (39.7mph)
Range: 370km (229 miles)
Vertical obstacle: 0.87m (2.8ft)
Trench crossing: 2.9m (9.5ft)
Fording: amphibious
Powerpack: Model 12150-L 12-cylinder diesel, developing 400 hp coupled to manual transmission.

29

Giat Industries Leclerc MBT

Giat describes the Leclerc as a 'third generation' MBT

The Leclerc MBT was developed for the French Army by Giat Industries, with the first prototype completed in 1989 and first production vehicles following in 1991. As well as being ordered by the French Army, in 1993 the United Arab Emirates ordered 388 Leclerc MBTs, two driver training tanks and 46 Armoured recovery vehicles. These have a number of modifications including a German powerpack.

The Leclerc has a three man crew, and a bustle-mounted automatic loader is fitted for the 120mm smooth bore gun, which holds 22 rounds of ready-use ammunition enabling a high rate of fire to be achieved. Other features include advanced passive armour over the frontal arc, passive day/night vision equipment for the commander, gunner and driver, as well as a computerised fire control system with stabilised sights for commander and gunner, a battlefield management system, an NBC (Nuclear, Biological, Chemical) system and deep fording capability. Mounted either side of the turret are nine launcher tubes which can fire various grenades.

Variants

Armoured recovery vehicle – longer hull and fitted with winch and crane

Armoured engineer vehicle – proposed design intended to have same hull as above

DTT – modified for driver training role

Specification

Crew: 3
Armament:
Main: 1 x 120mm gun
Co-axial: 1 x 12.7mm machine gun
Anti-aircraft: 1 x 7.62mm machine gun
Combat weight: 54,500kg (119,900lb)
Power-to-weight ratio: 27.52hp/t
Length with gun: 9.87m (32.4ft)
Hull length: 6.88m (22.6ft)

Width: 3.71m (12.2ft)
Height: 2.53m (8.3ft)
Ground clearance: 0.5m (1.6ft)
Maximum road speed: 71km/h (44mph)
Range: 550km (341 miles)
Vertical obstacle: 1.25m (4.1ft)
Trench crossing: 3m (9.8ft)
Fording: 1m (3.3ft)
Powerpack: SACM V8X-1500 x 8-cylinder Hyperbar diesel, developing 1500hp coupled to SESM ESM 500 automatic transmission.

Giat Industries AMX-30 B2 MBT

AMX-30Bs finally saw active service during the Gulf War

The AMX-30 was developed in the late 1950s for the French Army, with first production vehicles being completed at the now Giat Industries facility at Roanne in 1966. Production has now been completed, but it has started to be replaced in the French Army by the 120mm armed Leclerc MBT.

Standard equipment for the upgraded AMX-30 B2 MBT includes a computerised fire control system with a laser range-finder, an enhanced night vision system, a fire detection and suppression system, upgraded suspension, an improved powerpack, an NBC (Nuclear, Biological, Chemical) system and the ability to be fitted with a snorkel for deep fording. Some vehicles are now being fitted with explosive

reactive armour. The AMX-30S was developed
especially for export to the Middle East.

Variants

AMX-30S MBT (export only)
AMX-30D Armoured recovery vehicle
AMX-30 Armoured vehicle-launched bridge
AMX-30 combat engineer vehicle
AMX-30 mine clearing tank
AMX-30 SAM (Roland or Shahine)
AMX-30 twin 30mm self-propelled anti-aircraft gun
AMX-30 155mm GCT self-propelled gun
AMX-30 driver training tank

Specification

Crew: 4
Armament:
Main: 1 x 105mm gun
Co-axial: 1 x 12.7mm machine
gun
Anti-aircraft: 1 x 7.62mm
machine gun
Combat weight: 37,000kg
(81,400lb)
Power-to-weight ratio:
18.91hp/t
Length with gun: 9.48m (31.1ft)
Hull length: 6.59m (21.6ft)

Width: 3.1m (10.2ft)
Height: 2.86m (9.3ft)
Ground clearance: 0.44m (1.4ft)
Maximum road speed:
65km/h (40.3mph)
Range: 450km (279 miles)
Vertical obstacle: 0.93m (3.1ft)
Trench crossing: 2.9m (9.5ft)
Fording: 1.3m (4.3ft)
Powerpack: Hispano-Suiza HS
110 12-cylinder multi-fuel
developing 700hp coupled to
ENC 200 transmission.

33

Giat Industries AMX-13 Light Tank

The AMX-13 is used by many South American armies

The first prototype of the AMX-13 light tank was completed in 1948, with the first production vehicles completed by the now Giat Industries in 1952. The chassis of the AMX-13 light tank was subsequently used for a wide range of other vehicles including the AMX-VCI infantry fighting vehicle, 105mm and 155mm self-propelled guns.

First production vehicles were armed with a 75mm gun, but later versions had a 90mm or 105mm gun, although the latter was not adopted by the French Army. The AMX-13 has a unique oscillating turret with an upper part pivoting on a lower part. The gun is mounted in the upper turret, with the main armament fed by an automatic loader holding 12 rounds split between two revolver magazines.

The AMX-13 light tank was not initially fitted with an NBC (Nuclear, Biological, Chemical) system or night vision equipment, however some users have fitted the latter for the commander, gunner and driver, as well as a computerised fire control system including a laser range-finder, and a diesel engine.

Variants
Armoured vehicle-launched bridge
Armoured recovery vehicle
Multiple rocket launcher

Specification

Crew: 3
Armament:
Main: 1 x 90mm gun
Co-axial: 1 x 7.62mm machine gun
Anti-aircraft: 1 x 7.62mm machine gun
Combat weight: 15,000kg (33,000lb)
Power-to-weight ratio: 16.66bhp/t
Length with gun: 6.36m (20.8ft)
Hull length: 4.88m (16ft)

Width: 2.51m (8.2ft)
Height: 2.30m (7.5ft)
Ground clearance: 0.37m (1.3ft)
Maximum road speed: 60km/h (37.2mph)
Range: 400km (248 miles)
Vertical obstacle: 0.65m (0.4ft)
Trench crossing: 1.6m (5.2ft)
Fording: 0.6m (0.4ft)
Powerpack: Sofam Model 8Gxb 8-cylinder petrol, developing 250hp coupled to manual transmission.

Krauss-Maffei Leopard 2 MBT

The Leopard 2 is armed with a 120mm smoothbore gun

Following the cancellation of the German/United States MBT-70 tank, Germany went on to develop the Leopard 2 MBT from 1970, with the first prototypes armed with 105mm and 120mm guns. The 120mm version of the Leopard 2 was selected in 1977, with production undertaken by Krauss-Maffei and MaK, and first production vehicles completed in 1979. Since then, over 3,000 have been ordered and production was started again in 1994 for Sweden.

All Leopard 2 MBTs are armed with the 120mm smooth bore gun, which was later fitted to the United States M1A1/M1A2 MBTs, and have stabilised main armament, a computerised fire control system, day/thermal night sights, deep fording kit, a fire detection and suppression system and an NBC

(Nuclear, Biological, Chemical) system.

The German Army is to upgrade 225 of its Leopard 2s to the Leopard 2 (Improved) configuration which has a number of improvements including additional armour protection. This model is being built for Sweden as the Strv 122, while the ex German Army Leopard 2 are known as the Strv 121. The Swiss Leopard 2 is known as the Pz 87.

Variants
Armoured recovery vehicle
Driver training vehicle

Specification

Crew: 4

Armament:

Main: 1 x 120mm gun

Co-axial: 1 x 7.62mm machine gun;

Anti-aircraft: 1 x 7.62mm machine gun

Combat weight: 55,150kg (121,330lb)

Power-to-weight ratio: 27hp/t

Length with gun: 9.668m (31.7ft)

Hull length: 7.722m (25.3ft)

Width: 3.7m (12.13ft)

Height: 2.787m (9.1ft);

Ground clearance: 0.537m (1.8ft)

Maximum road speed: 72km/h (44.6mph)

Range: 550km (341 miles)

Vertical obstacle: 1.1m (3.6ft)

Trench crossing: 3m (9.8ft)

Fording: 1m (3.3ft)

Powerpack: MTU MB 873 Ka-501 12-cylinder diesel, developing 1500hp coupled to Renk HSWL 354 automatic transmission.

37

Krauss-Maffei Leopard 1A4 MBT

The Leopard 1 was sold to many other NATO armies

The Leopard 1 MBT was developed from the late 1950s, with first prototypes completed in 1960. Krauss-Maffei was selected as prime contractor for production, with first Leopard 1 MBTs completed in 1965. MaK was selected to manufacture specialised versions of the Leopard 1 MBT and also built some Leopard 1 MBTs.

All Leopard 1 MBTs are armed with the 105mm L7 series rifled tank gun and have the same powerpack. First production version was the Leopard 1, followed by the 1A2, 1A3 and 1A4, with the last two having welded turrets. Leopard 1s were subsequently upgraded to Leopard 1A1. Leopard 1A5 is the earlier Leopard 1, but with a computerised fire control system.

Standard equipment includes deep fording kit,

day/night vision equipment, a fire detection and suppression system and an NBC (Nuclear, Biological, Chemical) system. A dozer blade can also be mounted at the front. Many countries have local modifications including additional armour.

Variants
Armoured engineer vehicle
Armoured recovery vehicle
Armoured vehicle launched bridge
Driver training vehicle
Self-propelled anti-aircraft gun (2 x 35mm)

Specification

Crew: 4
Armament:
Main: 1 x 105mm gun
Co-axial: 1 x 7.62mm machine gun
Anti-aircraft: 1 x 7.62mm machine gun
Combat weight: 42,400kg (93,280lb)
Power-to-weight ratio: 19.57hp/t
Length with gun: 9.543m (31.3ft)
Hull length: 7.09m (23.3ft)
Width: 3.41m (11.2ft)

Height: 2.764m (9.1ft)
Ground clearance: 0.44m (1.44ft)
Maximum road speed: 65km/h (40.3mph)
Range: 600km (372 miles)
Vertical obstacle: 1.15m (3.8ft)
Trench crossing: 3m (9.8ft)
Fording: 2.25m (7.4ft)
Powerpack: MTU MB 838 Ca M-500 10-cylinder multi-fuel, developing 830hp coupled to ZF 4 HP 250 automatic transmission.

Thyssen Henschel TAM Tank

The TAM was built in Argentina to a German design

In the early 1970s the German company of Thyssen Henschel designed and built two vehicles for Argentina, the TAM medium tank and the VCI infantry combat vehicle. The prototypes were built in Germany with volume production being undertaken in Argentina by TAMSE. About 350 vehicles of both types being built. Both vehicles used some automotive components of the Marder 1 infantry combat vehicle employed by the German Army. The 105mm gun of the TAM fires standard NATO ammunition.

Standard equipment includes an NBC (Nuclear, Biological, Chemical) system and the ability to be fitted with long-range fuel tanks at the rear. For the export market Thyssen Henschel have developed the

TH 301 tank which has a number of improvements including stabilised sights for the commander and gunner, a computerised fire control system, a low light level TV camera mounted above the main armament, and a more powerful 750hp engine. The variants listed below were developed in Argentina.

Variants

VCRT (Armoured recovery vehicle)
VCA 155 (155mm self-propelled gun)
Multiple rocket launcher
VCI infantry combat vehicle

Specification

Crew: 4
Armament:
Main: 1 x 105mm gun
Co-axial: 1 x 7.62mm machine gun
Anti-aircraft: 1 x 7.62mm machine gun
Combat weight: 31,600kg (69,520lb)
Power-to-weight ratio: 22.78hp/t
Length with gun: 8.17m (26.8ft)
Hull length: 6.775m (22ft)

Width: 3.306m (10.8ft)
Height: 2.436m (8ft)
Ground clearance: 0.45m (1.5ft)
Maximum road speed: 76km/h (47mph)
Range: 550km (341 miles)
Vertical obstacle: 0.9m (3ft)
Trench crossing: 2.9m (9.5ft)
Fording: 1.4m (4.6ft)
Powerpack: MTU MB 833 Ka-500 6-cylinder diesel, developing 720hp coupled to Renk HSWL 204 transmission.

Merkava Mk3 MBT

Israeli combat experience led to the Merkava design

The Merkava was developed for the Israeli Armoured Corps and its design incorporates the lessons learned in the Arab-Israeli wars of 1967 and 1973. The first prototype was completed in 1974 and the first production Merkava Mk1 appeared in 1979. It was armed with the standard M68 105mm rifled gun. Further development resulted in the Merkava Mk2 which enterd service in late 1983. This has improved protection and carries a 60mm mortar in addition to the main armament. It also features a new transmission and an improved fire control system. Many Mk1s were brought up to Mk2 standard subsequently.

The current production model is the Mk3 which has many improvements including a 120mm smoothbore gun and better protection for the turret and hull. A new powerpack provides a better power to weight ratio and an upgraded suspension also increases its cross country performance.

Standard equipment on all Merkava MBTs includes a computerised fire control system with laser range-finder. The main armament is stablised in elevation and traverse and it has a full NBC (Nuclear, Biological, Chemical) defence system as well as night vision devices and a door in the hull rear for ammunition re-supply.

Variants
Slammer 155mm self-propelled gun (prototype)

Specification

Crew: 4
Armament:
Main: 1 x 120mm gun
Co-axial: 1 x 7.62mm machine gun
Anti-aircraft: 2 x 7.62mm machine guns
Mortar: 1 x 60mm mortar
Combat weight: 61,000kg (134,200lb)
Power-to-weight ratio: 19.67hp/t
Length with gun: 8.78m (28.8ft)

Length hull: 7.045m (23.1ft)
Width: 3.70m (12.1ft)
Height: 2.76m (9.1ft)
Ground clearance: 0.53m (1.7ft)
Maximum road speed: 55km/h (34mph)
Range: 500km (301 miles)
Vertical obstacle: 1.0m (3.28ft)
Fording: 1.38m (4.26ft)
Powerpack: Teledyne Continental AVDS 1790-9AR V-12 turbocharged diesel developing 1200hp coupled to Ashot automatic transmission.

IVECO/OTOBREDA C1 Ariete MBT

Italian tank battalions are now receiving the C1 Ariete

The C1 Ariete MBT has been developed by a consortium consisting of IVECO and OTOBREDA (previously OTO Melara), with the former responsible for the complete powerpack and suspension system, and OTOBREDA responsible for the chassis, turret, weapon system and final integration. A total of six prototypes have been built and the Italian Army has placed an order for a 200 vehicles, with production undertaken at the Le Spezia facility of OTOBREDA.

Main armament comprises a 120mm smooth bore gun fitted with a thermal sleeve, fume extractor and muzzle reference system which fires the same ammunition as the Leopard 2, Leclerc and M1A1/M1A2. The 120mm gun is fully stabilised in elevation and traverse and the computerised fire control system includes stabilised day/night sights for commander and gunner.

Standard equipment iincludes a fire detection/ suppression system, as well as an NBC (Nuclear, Biological, Chemical) system and provision for deep fording. Studies are currently underway on the C1 Ariete Mk 2 which will have a number of improvements including a more advanced fire control system, an automatic loader for the 20mm smooth bore gun, as well as hydro-pneumatic suspension, an 1500 hp diesel engine and increased armour for improved battlefield survivability.

Specification

Crew: 4
Armament:
Main: 1 x 120mm gun
Co-axial: 1 x 7.62mm machine gun;
Anti-aircraft: 1 x 7.62mm machine gun
Combat weight: 54,000 kg (118,800lb)
Power-to-weight ratio: 24.7hp/t
Length with gun: 9.669m (31.7ft)
Hull length: 7.59m (24.8ft)

Width: 3.601m (11.8ft)
Height: 2.5m (8.2ft)
Ground clearance: 0.44m (1.44ft)
Maximum road speed: 65 km/h (40.3mph)
Range: 550km (310 miles)
Vertical obstacle: 2.1m (6.9ft)
Trench crossing: 3.0m (9.8ft)
Fording: 1.2m (4ft)
Powerpack: VECO V-12 MTCA diesel, developing 1300hp coupled to ZF LSG 3000 automatic transmission.

45

OTO Breda OF-40 MBT

Developed privately, the OF-40 was sold to Dubai

The OF-40 was developed in the late 1970s by the then OTO Melara (now OTO Breda) and FIAT (now IVECO) for the export market, with the first prototype completed in 1980.

Dubai ordered two batches of OF-40 MBTs, 18 Mk 1s and 18 Mk 2, with the former subsequently upgraded to the Mk 2 standard, with a more advanced computerised fire control system, stabilised roof-mounted commanders for day/night panoramic sight and a low light level TV camera mounted above the mantlet of the 105 mm rifled tank gun.

Standard equipment includes a laser range-finder, a stabilisation system for the 105mm gun which fires standard NATO ammunition, an NBC (Nuclear, Biological, Chemical) system and deep fording

The chassis of the OF-40 MBT can be fitted with other turrets, for example a 76mm or twin 35mm radar-controlled anti-aircraft gun system. A modified OF-40 chassis with a different powerpack is used for the OTO Breda Palmaria 155mm self-propelled artillery system as developed for the export market. The projected OF-40/120 Mk 2A MBT is essentially an upgraded OF-40 chassis, with a 1000hp diesel and a turret similar to the new C1 Ariete MBT, but it is armed with a 120mm rifled tank gun.

Variants
OF-40 Armoured recovery vehicle

Specification

Crew: 4
Armament:
Main: 1 x 105mm gun
Co-axial: 1 x 7.62mm machine gun
Anti-aircraft: 1 x 7.62mm machine gun
Combat weight: 45,500kg (100,100lb)
Power-to-weight ratio: 18.24hp/t
Length with gun: 9.222m (30.5ft)

Hull length: 6.893m (22.6ft)
Width: 3.51m (11.5ft)
Height: 2.68m (8.8ft)
Ground clearance: 0.44m (1.4ft)
Maximum road speed: 60km/h (37.2mph)
Range: 600km (375 miles)
Vertical obstacle: 1.1m (3.6ft)
Trench crossing: 3m (9.8ft)
Fording: 1.2m (3.9ft)
Powerpack: MTU 10-cylinder multi-fuel, developing 830hp coupled to ZF transmission.

Mitsubishi Type 90 MBT

The Type 90 is armed with a 120 mm smoothbore gun

The Type 90 MBT was developed by Mitsubishi Heavy Industries from the mid-1970s under the designation of the STC, with the first two complete prototypes completed between 1982 and 1984. Following extensive trials with further modified prototypes, the vehicle was accepted for service as the Type 90 MBT, with the first order placed in 1990.

The Type 90 has a three man crew, and a bustle-mounted automatic loader is provided for the 120mm smooth bore gun which is essentially the German Rheinmetall weapon, as used in the Leopard 2 MBT and in a modified version in the US M1A1 and M1A2 MBTs. It is manufactured under licence in Japan.

Suspension of the Type 90 is of the hybrid type,

with torsion bars for the centre two road wheels and hydro-pneumatic units for the first and last road wheels, allowing the driver to adjust the ground clearance from 0.2 to 0.6m.

Standard equipment includes passive night vision equipment for commander, gunner and driver, a computerised fire control system, an all-electric gun control system and stabilisation system, and an NBC (Nuclear, Biological, Chemical) system. If required, a dozer blade can be mounted at the front of the hull.

Variants
Type 90 Armoured recovery vehicle

Specification

Crew: 3
Armament:
Main: 1 x 120mm gun
Co-axial: 1 x 7.62mm machine gun
Anti-aircraft: 1 x 12.7mm machine gun
Combat weight: 50,000kg (110,000lb)
Power-to-weight ratio: 30hp/t
Length with gun: 9.755m (32ft)
Hull length: 7.5m (24.6ft)

Width: 3.43m (11.3ft)
Height: 3.045m (10ft)
Ground clearance: 0.45m (1.5ft)
Maximum road speed: 70km/h (43.4mph)
Range: 400km (248 miles)
Vertical obstacle: 1.0m (3.3ft)
Trench crossing: 2.7m (7.3ft)
Fording: 1m (3.3ft)
Powerpack: Mitsubishi 10ZG 10-cylinder diesel, developing 1500hp coupled to automatic transmission.

49

Mitsubishi Type 74 MBT

The Type 74 has an adustable suspension

The Type 74 MBT was developed by Mitsubishi
Heavy Industries from the early 1960s as the
replacement for the 90 mm armed Type 61 MBT.

First prototypes were built in 1969 under the
designation of the STB and, following extensive trials
and further development work, the vehicle was
accepted for service as the Type 74 MBT. It is
estimated that a total of 873 Type 74 MBTs were
built for the Japanese Ground Self-Defence Force. It
has never been offered for export.

Standard equipment includes a computerised fire
control system, a stabilised 105 mm rifled tank gun
which fires all natures of ammunition including
APFSDS (Armour Piercing Fin Discarding Sabot) and

is fitted with fume extractor and thermal sleeve, an NBC (Nuclear, Biological, Chemical) system. A dozer blade can also be mounted at the front of the hull.

An unusual feature of the Type 74 MBT is its variable hydro-pneumatic suspension which allows it to be raised or lowered to enable the vehicle to have a ground clearance of between 200 to 650mm.

Variants

Type 78 Armoured recovery vehicle
Type 87 self-propelled anti-aircraft gun
Type 91 Armoured vehicle-launched bridge

Specification

Crew: 4
Armament:
Main: 1 x 105mm gun
Co-axial: 1 x 7.62mm machine gun
Anti-aircraft: 1 x 12.7mm machine gun
Combat weight: 38,000kg (83,600lb)
Power-to-weight ratio: 18.94hp/t
Length with gun: 9.42m (31ft)
Hull length: 6.7m (2.3ft)
Width: 3.18m (10.4ft)

Height: 2.67m (8.7ft)
Ground clearance: 0.2/0.65m (1.7/2.1ft)
Maximum road speed: 53km/h (32.9mph)
Range: 400km (248 miles)
Vertical obstacle: 1m (3.3ft)
Trench crossing: 2.7m (8.9ft)
Fording: 1m (3.3ft)
Powerpack: Mitsubishi 10ZFType 22 WT 10-cylinder diesel, developing 720hp coupled to Mitsubishi MT75A manual transmission.

51

Mitsubishi Type 61 MBT

Designed in the 1950s, the Type 61 is now obsolete

The Type 61 MBT was the first tank to be designed
in Japan after the end of the Second World War, with
production being undertaken by Mitsubishi Heavy
Industries. The first production Type 61 MBT was
completed in 1962 and a total of 560 vehicles were
built for the Japanese Ground Self Defence Force.
The Type 61 is now being phased out of service as the
more modern Type 90 MBT enter service.

By today's standards, the Type 61 is obsolete in the
four key areas of tank design, armour, mobility and
firepower. The main armament comprises a 90mm
rifled gun which is not stabilised, but which is fitted
with a fume extractor and a T type muzzle brake. The

commander has a cupola with an externally mounted 12.7mm machine gun which can be aimed and fired from within the vehicle. Some of these have been fitted with a shield. The Type 61 MBT has no computerised fire control system or NBC (Nuclear, Biological, Chemical) system.

Variants
Type 61 training tank
Type 70 Armoured recovery vehicle
Type 67 AEV
Type 67 Armoured vehicle-launched bridge

Specification

Crew: 4
Armament:
Main: 1 x 90mm gun
Co-axial: 1 x 7.62mm machine gun
Anti-aircraft: 1 x 12.7mm machine gun
Combat weight: 35,000kg (77,000lb)
Power-to-weight ratio: 17.14hp/t
Length with gun: 8.19m (26.9ft)
Hull length: 6.3m (20.7ft)

Width: 2.95m (9.7ft)
Height: 3.16m (10.36ft)
Ground clearance: 0.4m (1.3ft)
Maximum road speed: 45km/h (27.9mph)
Range: 200km (124 miles)
Vertical obstacle: 0.685m (2.2ft)
Trench crossing: 2.489m (8.1ft)
Fording: 0.99m (3.2ft)
Powerpack: Mitsubishi Type 12 HN 21 WT, V-12 turbo-charged diesel, developing 600hp coupled to manual transmission.

T-80U MBT

T-80Us now serve with the Russian and Chinese armies

The T-80 MBT was developed at the Kirov Works in Leningrad, with first production vehicles completed in the late 1970s.

Since it first entered service, the T-80 has been upgraded many times, with the latest T-80U having a more powerful gas turbine engine, and a significant increase in armour protection, with the 125mm smooth bore gun having the capability to fire a laser-guided missile out to a range of over 4000m. Early examples of the T-80 MBT were not fitted with explosive reactive armour (ERA). Like the T-64 and T-72, the T-80 has a three man crew, with the 125mm gun fed by an automatic loader.

Standard equipment includes an NBC (Nuclear, Biological, Chemical) system, a fire detection and suppression system, the ability to be fitted with a snorkel that allows it to ford to a depth of 6m. It also has night vision equipment for commander, gunner and driver.

Variants
T-80 (first model)
T-80B
T-80BK command tank
T-80BV with ERA
T-80BVK command tank with ERA
T-80U (turbine engine) -UD (diesel engine)

Specification
Crew: 3
Armament:
Main: 1 x 125mm gun
Co-axial: 1 x 7.66mm machine gun
Anti-aircraft: 1 x 12.7mm machine gun
Combat weight: 46,000kg (101,200lb)
Power-to-weight ratio: 27.20hp/t
Length with gun: 9.656m (31.7ft)
Hull length: 7m (23ft)

Width: 3.589m (11.8ft)
Height: 2.202m (7.2ft)
Ground clearance: 0.446m (1.5ft)
Maximum road speed: 70km/h (43mph)
Range: 335km (208 miles)
Vertical obstacle: 1m (3.3ft)
Trench crossing: 2.85m (9.4ft)
Fording: 1.2m (3.9ft)
Powerpack: Model GTD-1250 gas turbine, developing 1250hp coupled to manual transmisison.

T-72S MBT

T-72s were the best tanks available to Iraq in 1991

The T-72 MBT was developed at the Ural Tank Plant in Nizhnyi Tagil and entered production in 1971 with licence production being undertaken in Czechoslovakia, India, Iraq, Poland, Romania and Yugoslavia.

Like the T-64 and T-80, the T-72 has a three man crew with the 125mm gun being fed by an automatic loader. Since it first entered service, the T-72 has been upgraded many times, with the latest T-72S having a more powerful engine. It also has increased armour protection, with the 125mm smooth bore gun having the capability to fire a laser-guided missile out to a range of over 4000m. Some T-72 MBT have explosive reactive armour (ERA).

Standard equipment includes an NBC (Nuclear, Biological, Chemical) system, a fire detection and suppression system, as well as the ability to be fitted with a snorkel which allows it to ford to a depth of 5m. It also has night vision equipment for the commander, gunner and driver, and provision for mounting various types of mine clearing and dozer blades at the front of the hull.

Variants

There are many variants of the basic T-72 MBT; command models are the T-72K

MTU-72 Armoured vehicle-launched bridge

BREM-1 Armoured recovery vehicle

IMR-2 combat engineer vehicle

Specification

Crew: 3
Armament:
Main: 1 x 125mm gun
Co-axial: 1 x 7.62mm machine gun
Anti-aircraft: 1 x 12.7mm machine gun
Combat weight: 44,500kg (97,900lb)
Power-to-weight ratio: 18.9hp/t
Length with gun: 9.53m (31ft)
Hull length: 6.95m (22.8ft)

Width: 3.59m (11.8ft)
Height: 2.222m (7.3ft)
Ground clearance: 0.49m (1.6ft)
Maximum road speed: 60km/h (37mph)
Range: 480km (278 miles)
Vertical obstacle: 0.85m (2.8ft)
Trench crossing: 2.8m (9.2ft)
Fording: 1.8m (6ft)
Powerpack: V-84 V-12 diesel, developing 840hp coupled to hydraulically assisted transmission.

T-64B MBT

The T-64 was never exported within the Warsaw Pact.

The T-64 MBT was developed in the late 1960s, with first production examples fitted with the 115mm smooth bore gun of the T-62 fed by an automatic loader. The T-64 was never exported, even to members of the former Warsaw Pact. The main production T-64A was accepted for service in 1969.

It is fitted wth a 125mm smooth bore gun fed by an automatic loader, which has enabled the tank crew to be reduced to three men: commander, gunner and driver. Since it first entered service, the T-64 has been upgraded many times, with the T-64B having improved armour protection and a computerised fire control system allowing it to fire the AT-8 Songster radio-guided missile out to a range of 4000m. More recently, the T-64 MBT has been fitted with explosive reactive armour on its hull and turret for improved battlefield survivability.

Standard equipment includes an NBC (Nuclear, Biological, Chemical) system, a fire detection and suppression system, the ability to be fitted with a snorkel allowing it to ford to a depth of 5m, as well as night vision equipment for commander, gunner and driver, and provision for mounting various types of mine-clearing devices or dozer blades.

Variants
T-64AK command tank
T-64B series MBT
T-64R MBT

Specification

Crew: 3
Armament:
Main: 1 x 125mm gun
Co-axial: 1 x 7.62mm machine gun
Anti-aircraft: 1 x 12.7mm machine gun
Combat weight: 39,500kg (86,900lb)
Power-to-weight ratio: 17.7hp/t
Length with gun: 9.9m (32.5ft)
Hull length: 7.4m (24.3ft)

Width: 3.38m (11.1ft)
Height: 2.2m (7.2ft)
Ground clearance: 0.37m (1.2ft)
Maximum road speed: 75km/h (46.5mph)
Range: 400km (248 miles)
Vertical obstacle: 0.8m (2.6ft)
Trench crossing: 2.28m (7.5ft)
Fording: 1.8m (6ft)
Powerpack: 5DTF 5-cylinder diesel, developing 700hp coupled to power-assisted transmission.

T-62 MBT

T-62s were widely used in the 1973 Arab-Israeli war

The T-62 MBT was developed at Nizhnyi Tagil from the earlier T-55 MBT and, following trials, was accepted for service in 1962. It was first seen in public in 1965. It was also built in Czechoslovakia for the export market.

From 1967 a number of improvements were carried out: a 12.7mm anti-aircraft machine gun was added to the loader's position, armour protection was increased and a fire control system fitted. It was modified to fire the *Sheksna* (US designation AT-10) laser beam riding missile out to a range of 5000m.

Standard equipment includes an NBC (Nuclear,

Biological, Chemical) system, a fire detection and suppression system, as well as the facility to be fitted with a snorkel allowing it to ford to a depth of 5m, also night vision equipment for commander, gunner and driver, and the ability to lay smoke screen by injecting diesel fuel into the exhaust on the left side of the hull.

Variants

T-62D series with *Drozd* anti-missile system
T-62K command tank
T-62M series with AT-10
T-62 flame-thrower

Specification

Crew: 4
Armament:
Main: 1 x 115mm gun
Co-axial: 1 x 7.62mm machine gun
Anti-aircraft: 1 x 12.7mm (T-62M)
Combat weight: 40,000 kg (88,000lb)
Power-to-weight ratio: 14.5hp/t
Length with gun: 9.335m (30.6ft)
Hull length: 6.63m (21.7ft)

Width: 3.3m (10.8ft)
Height: 2.395m (7.9ft)
Ground clearance: 0.43m (1.4ft)
Maximum road speed: 50km/h (31mph)
Range: 450km (279 miles)
Vertical obstacle: 0.8m (2.6ft)
Trench crossing: 2.85m (9.3ft)
Fording: 1.4m (4.6ft)
Powerpack: V-55-5 V-12 diesel, developing 580hp coupled to manual transmission.

T-54/55 MBT

The T-54/55 has been manufactured in vast numbers

The T-54 MBT was developed shortly after the end of the Second World War, with the first prototypes being completed in 1946 and first production examples in 1947. It is estimated that over 50,000 T-54/T-55 tanks were built, with production being completed in 1981. It was built in China (as the Type 59), Czechoslovakia and Poland.

The T-54 was followed by the improved T-55. Both are armed with a 100mm gun, but there have been many sub-variants and local modifications. Some vehicles have a new fire control system and additional armour. Some Egyptian vehicles also have a British

105mm L7 rifled tank gun.

Standard equipment includes an NBC (Nuclear, Biological, Chemical) system, a fire detection and suppression system, as well as the ability to be fitted with a snorkel, night vision equipment for commander, gunner and driver, and the ability to lay smoke screen by injecting diesel fuel into the exhaust.

Variants
Armoured recovery vehicle
Armoured vehicle-launched bridge
Engineer vehicle
Flame thrower

Specification

Crew: 4
Armament:
Main: 1 x 100mm gun
Bow: 1 x 7.62mm machine gun
Co-axial: 1 x 7.62mm machine gun
Anti-aircraft: 1 x 12.7mm
Combat weight: 36,000kg (79,200lb)
Power-to-weight ratio: 14.44hp/t
Length with gun: 9m (29.5ft)
Hull length: 6.04m (19.8ft)

Width: 3.27m (10.7ft)
Height: 2.75m (9ft)
Ground clearance: 0.425m (1.4ft)
Maximum road speed: 50km/h (31mph)
Range: 510km (318 miles)
Vertical obstacle: 0.8m (2.6ft)
Trench crossing: 2.7m (8.9ft)
Fording: 1.4m (4.6ft)
Powerpack: V-54 V-12 diesel, developing 520 hp coupled to manual transmission.

T-34/85 Medium Tank

World War II T-34 s are still serving in former-Yugoslavia

The first model of the T-34 medium tank entered service with the Russian Army in 1940 and was armed with a 76mm gun. The T-34/85 medium tank entered service in 1943 and was armed with a long-barrelled 85mm gun. Production of this continued in Russia until 1948. In the post Second World War period, the T-34/85 was also manufactured in the former Czechoslovakia and Poland. The T-34/85 medium tank has seen considerable combat use in such conflicts as Korea, Middle East and Africa. It no longer remains in service with the major armies, but is still used as a frontline MBT by a number of countries in Africa and Asia.

The layout of the T-34 is conventional, with the driver front left and bow machine gunner to his right, a three man turret in the centre and an engine compartment at the rear. The vehicle is not fitted with an NBC (Nuclear, Biological, Chemical) system or night vision equipment, but its operational range can be extended with the use of long-range fuel tanks mounted either side of the hull rear.

Variants
Armoured recovery vehicle (numerous versions)
Armoured vehicle-launched bridge
Dozer tanks

Specification

Crew: 5
Armament:
Main: 1 x 85mm gun
Bow: 1 x 7.62mm machine gun
Co-axial: 1 x 7.62mm machine gun
Combat weight: 32,000kg (70,400lb)
Power-to-weight ratio: 15.62hp/t
Length with gun: 8.076m (26.5ft)
Hull length: 6.19m (20.3ft)

Width: 2.997m (9.8ft)
Height: 2.743m (9ft)
Ground clearance: 0.38m (1.2ft)
Maximum road speed: 55km/h (34.1mph)
Range: 300km (186 miles)
Vertical obstacle: 0.73m (2.4ft)
Trench crossing: 2.5m (8.2ft)
Fording: 1.32m (4.3ft)
Powerpack: V-2-34 V-12 diesel, developing 500hp coupled to manual transmission

PT-76 Light Tank

Despite its size, the PT-76 is very lightly armoured

The PT-76 light amphibious tank was developed shortly after the end of the Second World War and accepted for service in 1950. It is estimated that about 7,000 vehicles were built, with final deliveries taking place in the early 1960s.

The first production version had an 76mm gun fitted with the D-56T gun with a multi-slotted muzzle brake. The most common version has a number of improvements including the installation of the 76mm D-56TM gun which has a double-baffle muzzle brake and a bore evacuator near the muzzle.

The PT-76B has the 76mm D-56TS gun which is stabilised.

Standard equipment includes night vision equipment, and some vehicles are fitted with an NBC (Nuclear, Biological, Chemical) system. To extend the operational range of the PT-76, additional fuel drums can be fitted on the rear of the hull. The PT-76 is fully amphibious, propelled in the water by two water-jets mounted at the rear of the hull. Before entering the water, the trim vane is erected at the front of the hull and the bilge pumps are switched on.

The Chinese have a similar version called the Type 63 but this has a different turret.

Specification

Crew: 3
Armament:
Main: 1 x 76.2mm gun
Co-axial: 1 x 7.62mm machine gun
Anti-aircraft: 1 x 12.7mm machine gun (optional)
Combat weight: 14,600kg (32,120lb)
Power-to-weight ratio: 16.4hp/t
Length with gun: 7.66m (25.1ft)
Hull length: 7.22m (23.7ft)

Width: 3.17m (10.4ft)
Height: 2.255m (7.4ft)
Ground clearance: 0.34m (1.1ft)
Maximum road speed: 44km/h (27.3mph)
Range: 400km (248 miles)
Vertical obstacle: 1.1m (3.6ft)
Trench crossing: 2.8m (9.2ft)
Fording: amphibious
Powerpack: Model V-6B 6-cylinder diesel, developing 240hp coupled to manual transmission.

Hyundai Type 88 MBT

The Type 88 was first developed by General Dynamics

The Type 88 MBT, also referred to as the K-1, was developed by the now General Dynamics Land Systems Division for the South Korean Army, with the first prototypes completed in the United States in 1983. Production commenced in South Korea by the Hyundai Precision machine gun Ind Company in 1984, with first production vehicles being comepleted in 1985.

Main armament comprises the combat-proven 105mm M68 rifled tank gun which is fully stabilised in elevation and traverse. The computerised fire control system includes a gunner's stabilised day/thermal night sight with laser range-finder, while the commander has a roof-mounted stabilised panoramic sight. The suspension is adjustable, which allows the main armament to be depressed to -10 degrees, and there is also a remote track adjusting system. The hull and turret incorporate advanced composite armour for improved battlefield survivability. Standard equipment includes fording kit, fire detection and suppression system and NBC (Nuclear, Biological, Chemical) system.

Variants
Armoured recovery vehicle
Armoured vehicle launched bridge

Specification

Crew: 4
Armament:
Main: 1 x 105mm gun
Co-axial: 1 x 7.62mm machine gun
Anti-aircraft: 1 x 12.7mm machine gun (commander)
Anti-aircraft: 1 x 7.62mm machine gun (loader)
Combat weight: 51,000kg (112,200lb)
Power-to-weight ratio: 23.5hp/t
Length with gun: 9.672m (31.7ft)

Hull length: 7.477m (24.5ft)
Width: 3.594m (11.8ft)
Height: 2.248m (7.4ft)
Ground clearance: 0.46m (1.5ft)
Maximum road speed: 65km/h (40.3mph)
Range: 500km (310 miles)
Vertical obstacle: 1m (3.3ft)
Trench crossing: 2.74m (9ft)
Fording: 1.20m (3.9ft)
Powerpack: MTU 871 Ka-501 diesel, developing 1200hp coupled to ZF LSG 3000 automatic transmission.

Bofors Stridsvagn 103C MBT

Sweden's distinctive turretless S-tank on manoeuvres

The S-tank was developed from the late 1950s by Bofors for the Swedish Army and, following trials with prototype vehicles, a total of 300 production S-tanks were delivered to the Swedish Army between 1966 and 1971.

Since it entered service with the Swedish Army, the S-tank has been constantly updated with the latest Strv 103C, and has many improvements including the replacement of the Rolls-Royce K60 engine by the Detroit Diesel, as well as modified transmission, a laser range-finder and additional fuel tanks. The main armament is a 105mm rifled tank gun fed by an automatic loader mounted at the rear of the hull. The 105mm gun is aimed by the driver in elevation by raising or lowering the suspension, while in traverse it is laid by traversing the complete chassis. Mounted, collapsed around the top of the hull, is a floatation screen and, when erected, the S-tank is propelled in the water by its tracks at a maximum speed of 6 km/h. While there are no variants of the S-tank, some components of the vehicle are used in the Bofors Bandkanon 155mm self-propelled artillery system which is only in service with the Swedish Army.

Specification

Crew: 3
Armament:
Main: 1 x 105mm gun
Co-axial: 2 x 7.62mm machine gun
Anti-aircraft: 1 x 7.62mm machine gun
Combat weight: 39,500 kg (86,900lb)
Power-to-weight ratio: 19.74hp/t
Length with gun: 8.99m (29.5ft)
Hull length: 7.04m (23.1ft)

Width: 3.63m (11.9ft)
Height: 2.43m (8ft)
Ground clearance: 0.50m (1.6ft)
Maximum road speed: 50km/h (31mph)
Range: 390km (241 miles)
Vertical obstacle: 0.9m (3ft)
Trench crossing: 2.3m (7.5ft)
Fording: 1.5m (5ft)
Powerpack: Detroit Diesel Model 6V-53T, developing 290hp and Boeing 553 gas turbine, developing 490 shp, coupled to Volvo transmission.

Hagglunds Vehicle Ikv-91 Tank Destroyer

The Ikv-91 tank destroyer is designed for arctic warfare

The Ikv-91 full-tracked tank destroyer was developed by Hagglunds Vehicle for the Swedish Army. The first prototype was completed in 1969, with the main production run being carried out between 1975 and 1978. The vehicle was never exported and is no longer being marketed.

The Ikv-91 uses some automotive components of the Hagglunds Vehicle Pbv 302 full-tracked armoured personnel carrier. The layout of the vehicle is conventional, with the driver at the front, a turret in the centre and powerpack at the rear. Main armament comprises a 90mm gun fitted with a thermal sleeve and fume extractor, firing fin-stabilised HE and

HEAT (High Explosive Anti-Tank) projectiles. A
7.62mm machine gun is mounted co-axially, with the
main armament with a 7.62mm machine gun
mounted on the loader's cupola. A bank of six smoke
grenade dischargers are mounted either side of the
turret. The fire control system includes a laser range-
finder. With preparation, the Ikv-91 is fully
amphibious, propelled in the water by its tracks at a
maximum speed of 6.5km/h. Standard equipment
includes flare launchers, an NBC (Nuclear, Biological,
Chemical) system and a HEAT (High Explosive Anti-
Tank).

Specification

Crew: 4
Armament:
Main: 1 x 90mm gun
Co-axial: 1 x 7.62mm machine
gun
Anti-aircraft: 1 x 7.62mm
machine gun
Combat weight: 16,300kg
(35,860lb)
Power-to-weight ratio:
22.2hp/t
Length with gun: 8.84m
(28.9ft)
Hull length: 6.41m (21ft)

Width: 3m (9.8ft)
Height: 2.32m (7.6ft)
Ground clearance: 0.37m (1.2ft)
Maximum road speed:
65km/h (40.3mph)
Range: 500km (310 miles)
Vertical obstacle: 0.8m (2.6ft)
Trench crossing: 2.8m (9.2ft)
Fording: amphibious
Powerpack: Volvo Penta TD
120 A 6-cylinder turbocharged
diesel, developing 330hp
coupled to Allison automatic
transmission.

73

Pz 68 MBT

Pz 68: the first and last tank designed and built entirely in Switzerland

The first Swiss designed and built MBT was the Pz 61. A total of 150 were built between 1965 and 1966, but they are to be phased out of service by the Swiss Army from 1995. Further development of the Pz 61 resulted in the Pz 68 which, similar in appearance, is also armed with a 105mm rifled tank gun. A total of 390 Pz 68 MBT in four different batches (Mk 1, 2, 3 and 4) were built between 1971 and 1984.

As built ,the Pz 68 was not fitted with a computerised fire control system, but some of these have now been upgraded by the installation of a computerised fire control system, a stabilised sighting system for the gunner, a muzzle reference system, an improved suspension and an NBC (Nuclear, Biological, Chemical) system. When upgraded, the vehicle is known as the Pz 68/88. The Pz 68 was the last MBT to be designed and built in Switzerland, followed by local production of the German Leopard 2 under the designation of the Pz 87 Leo.

Variants
Bru Pz 68 Armoured vehicle-launched bridge
Entp Pz 65 Armoured recovery vehicle
Pz Zielfz target tank

Specification

Crew: 4
Armament:
Main: 1 x 105mm gun
Co-axial: 1 x 7.5mm machine gun
Anti-aircraft: 1 x 7.5mm machine gun
Power-to-weight ratio: 16.62hp/t
Length with gun: 9.49m (31.1ft)
Hull length: 6.88m (22.6ft)
Width: 3.14m (33.8ft)

Height: 2.88m (9.5ft)
Ground clearance: 0.41m (1.3ft)
Maximum road speed: 55km/h (34.1mph)
Range: 350km (217 miles)
Vertical obstacle: 0.75m (2.5ft)
Trench crossing: 2.6m (8.5ft)
Fording: 1.1m (3.6ft)
Powerpack: MTU MB 837 Ba-500 8-cylinder diesel, developing 660hp coupled to SLM semi-automatic transmission.

75

Vickers Challenger 2 MBT

The Challenger 2 is now in full production for the British Army and Oman

Further development of the Challenger 1 by Vickers Defence Systems resulted in the Challenger 2 MBT, of which 386 have been ordered by the British Army, with deliveries running from 1994 through to 2,000. Oman has ordered 18 Challenger 2 MBTs. With the introduction of Challenger 2, all remaining Chieftain and Challenger 1 MBTs will be phased out of service with the British Army.

Although similar in appearance to Challenger 1, the Challenger 2 MBT has many improvements including a brand new turret armed with the latest 120mm L30 rifled tank gun firing a new APFSDS-T (Armour Piercing Fin Discarding Sabot Tracer) projectile with a depleted uranium penetrator. The new computerised fire control system, all electric gun control and stabilising system, and stabilised sights for the commander and gunner give a high degree of first round hit probability under both day and night conditions.

Standard equipment includes a thermal camera over the manlet of the 120mm gun which provides a picture for gunner and commander, as well as an NBC (Nuclear, Biological, Chemical) system, mounting points for additional fuel drums at the rear, and mounting points for a Combat Dozer Blade at the front of the hull.

Specification

Crew: 4
Armament:
Main: 1 x 120mm gun
Co-axial: 1 x 7.62mm machine gun
Anti-aircraft: 1 x 7.62mm machine gun
Combat weight: 62,500kg (137,500lb)
Power-to-weight ratio: 19.2hp/t
Length with gun: 11.55m (37.9ft)
Hull length: 8.327m (27.3ft)
Width: 3.52m (11.5ft)
Height: 2.49m (8.17ft)

Ground clearance: 0.50m (1.6ft)
Maximum road speed: 56km/h (34.8mph)
Range: 450km (279 miles)
Vertical obstacle: 0.9m (3ft)
Trench crossing: 2.34m (7.7ft)
Fording: 1.07m (3.5ft)
Powerpack: Perkins Engines (Shrewsbury) Condor V-12 1200 12-cylinder diesel, developing 1200hp coupled to David Brown Vehicle Transmissions TN54 transmission.

Vickers Challenger 1 MBT

Challenger 1 tanks were used with great success by the British in the Gulf War

The Challenger 1 was developed from the Shir 2 MBT which was originally developed by the then Royal Armament Research and Development Establishment at Chertsey for Iran. Production of the Challenger 1 was undertaken at the Royal Ordnance Factory Leeds (now owned by Vickers Defence Systems), with a total of 420 vehicles being delivered to the British Army between 1983 and 1990. The 120mm rifled tank gun is the same as that installed in the Chieftain MBT, and the computerised fire control system, which includes a laser range-finder, is also similar.

Standard equipment includes day/thermal sights for commander and gunner, a stabilisation system for a 120mm gun, an NBC (Nuclear, Biological, Chemical) system, as well as mounting points for additional fuel drums at the rear, and mounting points for a Combat Dozer Blade at the front of the hull.

For operations in the Middle East, such as Operation Desert Storm, the Challenger 1 was upgraded in a number of key areas including the installation of explosive reactive armour at the front of the hull, and passive Chobham armour skirts.

Variants
CR ARRV – Challenger Armoured Repair and Recovery Vehicle
CTT – Challenger Training Tank

Specification

Crew: 3
Armament:
Main: 1 x 120mm gun
Co-axial: 1 x 7.62mm machine gun
Anti-aircraft: 1 x 7.62mm machine gun
Combat weight: 62,000kg (136,400lb)
Power-to-weight ratio: 19.35bhp/t
Length with gun: 11.56m (37.9ft)
Hull length: 8.327m (27.3ft)
Width: 3.518m (11.5ft)

Height: 2.95m (9.7ft)
Ground clearance: 0.5m (1.6ft)
Maximum road speed: 56km/h (34.8mph)
Range: 450km (279 miles)
Vertical obstacle: 0.9m (3ft)
Trench crossing: 2.8m (9.2ft)
Fording: 1.07m (3.5ft)
Powerpack: Perkins Engines (Shrewsbury) Condor V-12 1200 12-cylinder diesel, developing 1200hp coupled to David Brown Vehicle Transmissions TN37 transmission

Vickers Chieftain MBT

The Chieftain was the main British MBT for over 30 years

The Chieftain MBT was developed from the late
1950s as the replacement for the Centurion MBT, with
production being undertaken at Royal Ordnance
Factory Leeds (taken over by Vickers Defence Systems
in 1986) and Vickers Defence Systems at Newcastle
Upon Tyne.

As built, the Chieftain was not fitted with a fire
control system, and used a 12.7mm ranging machine
gun to range onto the target. When tracer rounds were
observed striking the target, the appropriate corrections
were applied to the 120mm gun. British Army
Chieftain MBTs were subsequently fitted with a laser
range-finder, a computerised fire control system,
thermal night sights and additional armour protection.

The 120mm rifled tank gun fires seperate loading ammunition (projectile and charge), and is the same as that installed in the Challenger 1 MBT. Standard equipment includes mounting points for a dozer blade at the hull and an NBC (Nuclear, Biological, Chemical) system.

Variants
Chieftain Armoured recovery vehicle
Chieftain Armoured Vehicle Royal Engineer
Chieftain Armoured Vehicle Launched Bridge
Chieftain Repair and Recovery Vehicle

Specification

Crew: 4
Armament:
Main: 1 x 120mm gun
Co-axial: 1 x 7.62mm machine gun
Anti-aircraft: 1 x 7.62mm machine gun
Combat weight: 55,000kg (12,100lb)
Power-to-weight ratio: 13.63 bhp/t
Length with gun: 10.975m (36ft)
Hull length: 7.518m (24.7ft)
Width: 3.504m (11.5ft)

Height: 2.895m (9.5ft)
Ground clearance: 0.508m (1.67ft)
Maximum road speed: 48km/h (29.8mph)
Range: 400–500km (250-312 miles)
Vertical obstacle: 0.914m (3ft)
Trench crossing: 3.149m (10.3ft)
Fording: 1.066m (3.5ft)
Powerpack: Leyland L60 multi-fuel, developing 750bhp coupled to TN12 transmission.

Centurion Mk 13 MBT

Centurion tanks of the South African Defence Force

The Centurion MBT was developed towards the end of the Second World War, with production undertaken by Vickers Defence Systems, Leyland Motors and the Royal Ordnances Factories at Woolwich and Leeds. A total of 4423 Centurions were built, with production completed in 1962. Although replaced in the British Army service by the Chieftain, the Centurion still remains in service in a number of countries today.

First examples had a 17-pounder (76.2mm gun); followed by the 20-pounder (83.8mm) and, finally, the famous L7 105mm gun, subsequently fitted to many other vehicles including the Leopard 1,

M48A5, Merkava Mk 1 and Mk 2, M60/M60A1, and the M1 and Type 88 MBTs, to name but a few. Some have fitted their vehicles with a fire control system and passive night vision equipment as part of a complete rebuild which also includes new armour (Israel and South Africa, for example).

There are at least 13 basic marks of the Centurion, with many sub-variants and local modifications.

Variants
Armoured recovery vehicle
Armoured vehicle-launched bridge

Specification

Crew: 4
Armament:
Main: 1 x 105mm gun (ranging): 1 x 12.7mm machine gun
Co-axial: 1 x 7.62mm machine gun
Anti-aircraft: 1 x 7.62mm machine gun
Combat weight: 51,820kg (114,004ft)
Power-to-weight ratio: 12.54hp/t
Length with gun: 9.854m (32.3ft)

Hull length: 7.823m (25.7ft)
Width: 3.39m (11.1ft)
Height: 3.009m (9.9ft)
Ground clearance: 0.51m (1.7ft)
Maximum road speed: 34.6km/h (21.5mph)
Range: 190km (118miles)
Vertical obstacle: 0.914m (3ft)
Trench crossing: 3.352m (11ft)
Fording: 1.45m (4.8ft)
Powerpack: Rolls-Royce Mk IVB Meteor 12-cylinder petrol, developing 650hp coupled to Z51R manual transmission.

Vickers Mk 3 MBT

Vickers developed the Mk3 MBT as a private venture

In the late 1950s the now Vickers Defence Systems developed the Vickers Mk 1 MBT for the Indian Army. It was armed with a 105mm gun, powered by a Leyland L60 engine and had a welded hull and turret.

The Mk 1 was subsequently manufactured in India, as the Vijayanta, and India has also built its own specialised versions including an Armoured recovery vehicle, the Armoured vehicle-launched bridge and a 130 mm self-propelled gun, with the latter two versions having a stretched chassis with seven road wheels. Between 1970 and 1972 Kuwait took delivery of 70 Vickers Mk 1 MBTs.

Further development resulted in the much improved Mk 3 which has a new cast turret, a computerised fire control system which includes a laser range-finder, an all-electric gun control and stabilisation system, day/night sights and an NBC (Nuclear, Biological, Chemical) system. Main armament comprises a 105 mm L7 gun, firing standard NATO ammunition.

Variants
Armoured vehicle-launched bridge
Armoured recovery vehicle

Specification

Crew: 4
Armament:
Main: 1 x 105mm gun
(ranging): 1 x 12.7mm machine gun
Co-axial: 1 x 7.62mm machine gun
Anti-aircraft: 1 x 12.7mm machine gun
Combat weight: 40,000kg (88,000lb)
Power-to-weight ratio: 18bhp/t
Length with gun: 9.788m (32.1ft)
Hull length: 7.561m (24.8ft)

Width: 3.168m (10.4ft)
Height: 3.099m (10.2ft)
Ground clearance: 0.432m (1.42ft)
Maximum road speed: 50km/h (31mph)
Range: 530km (327 miles)
Vertical obstacle: 0.83m (2.7ft)
Trench crossing: 3m (9.9ft)
Fording: 1.1m (3.6ft)
Powerpack: Detroit Diesel Model 12V-71T turbo-charged diesel, developing 720 bhp coupled to Self-Changing Gears TN12 semi-automatic transmission

Alvis Scorpion Light Tank

The tiny Scorpion carries a 76 mm or 90 mm gun

The Combat Vehicle Reconnaissance (Tracked) family of vehicles was developed by Alvis for the British Army. First prototypes were completed in 1969, with first production vehicles following in 1972. By 1995 over 3,500 had been built for the home and export markets.

The hull and turret is of all-welded aluminium, with the driver front left, the engine to his right and the two man turret at the rear. The basic Scorpion is armed with a 76mm gun, although this version has been phased out of service with the British Army. Late production vehicles have a diesel engine, with the option of a 90mm gun and various fire control systems. When the flotation screen is erected, the

Scorpion is fully amphibious, propelled in the water by its tracks at a speed of 6.5km/h. Standard equipment includes NBC (Nuclear, Biological, Chemical) system, fire detection and suppression system and night vision equipment.

Variants
Scorpion 90mm
Spartan and Stormer armoured personnel carriers
Spartan and Striker tank destroyers
Samaritan ambulance
Sultan command vehicle
Samson ambulance
Scimitar and Sabre 30mm

Specification

Crew: 3
Armament:
Main: 1 x 76mm gun
Co-axial: 1 x 7.62mm machine gun
Combat weight: 8,073kg (17,760.6lb)
Power-to-weight ratio: 23.54bhp/t
Hull length: 4.794m (15.7ft)
Width: 2.235m (7.3ft)
Height: 2.102m (6.9ft)

Ground clearance: 0.35m (1.2ft)
Maximum road speed: 80.5km/h (49.9mph)
Range: 644km (399 miles)
Vertical obstacle: 0.5m (1.6ft)
Trench crossing: 2.057m (6.7ft)
Fording: 1.067m (3.5ft)
Powerpack: Jaguar J60 No 1 Mk 100B 6-cylinder petrol, developing 190hp coupled to TN15 semi-automatic transmission.

General Dynamics M1A1 MBT

The M1 Abrams first saw action during the 1991 Gulf War

The M1 Abrams MBT was developed by the Chrysler Corporation (now General Dynamics Land Systems Division) with the first prototypes being completed in 1976. The first production model was the M1 and was armed with the same M68 105mm rifled gun fitted to the earlier M60 series. The Improved M1 which followed has increased armour protection.

The first production M1A1 appeared in 1985. This has many improvements including additional armour, a 120mm Rheinmetall smoothbore gun, better NBC (Nuclear, Biological, Chemical) defensive measures and an unrated suspension. Late production models have depleted uranium armour.

The final production version is the M1A2 which has

all the improvements of the M1A1 plus a commander's independent thermal viewer. Standard equipment on all the M1 series includes computerised fire control system, stablised sights and main armament.

Variants
Armoured Recovery Vehicle (prototype)
Armoured Engineer Vehicle (prototype)
Armoured Vehicle-launched Bridge (prototype)

Specification

Crew: 4
Armament:
Main: 1 x 120mm gun
Co-axial: 1 x 7.62mm machine gun
Anti-aircraft: 1 x 7.62mm machine gun
Anti-aircraft: 1 x 7.62mm machine gun
Combat weight: 57,154kg (125,738lbs)
Power-to-weight ratio: 26.24hp/t
Length with gun: 9.828m (32.24ft)
Length hull: 7.918m (25.97ft)
Width: 3.657m (11.99ft)

Height: 2.886m (9.46ft)
Ground Clearance: 0.482m (1.58ft)
Maximum road speed: 67km/h (41.6mph)
Range: 465km (289 miles)
Vertical obstacle: 1.066m (3.49ft)
Trench crossing: 2.743m (8.99ft)
Fording: 1.219m (3.99ft)
Powerpack: Textron Lycoming AGT 1500 gas turbine developing 1500hp coupled to Allison Transmission X-1100-3B automatic transmission.

General Dynamics M60A3 MBT

The M60 was the main Israeli tank during the 1970s

The M60 MBT was a further development of the earlier 90mm armed M48 MBT, with the most significant improvement being the installation of a 105mm rifled tank gun and a diesel engine. The M60 entered service with the United States Army in 1960, and was followed in production two years later by the M60A1 which had a number of improvements including a brand new turret with greater ballistic protection.

The final production model was the M60A3 which has a stabilisation system for the main armament, a more reliable powerpack and smoke grenade dischargers. The M60A3 TTS (Tank Thermal Sight) also has a fire control computer and laser range-finder for improved first round hit probabilty. Although the M60 series has been phased out of front-line service with the United States Army and many are being passed on, some countries to receive them, for example Israel, have carried out many improvements to the M60 series including the installation of passive or active armour packages for improved battlefield survivability.

Variants
M60 Armoured vehicle-launched bridge
M728 Combat Engineer Vehicle

Specification

Crew: 4
Armament:
Main: 1 x 105mm gun
Co-axial: 1 x 7.62mm machine gun
Anti-aircraft: 1 x 12.7mm machine gun
Combat weight: 52,617kg (115,757lb)
Power-to-weight ratio: 14.24bhp/t
Length with gun: 9.436m (31ft)
Hull length: 6.946m (22.8ft)

Width: 3.631m (11.9ft)
Height: 3.27m (10.7ft)
Ground clearance: 0.45m (1.5ft)
Maximum road speed: 48.28km/h (30mph)
Range: 480km (297 miles)
Vertical obstacle: 0.914m (3ft)
Trench crossing: 2.59m (22ft)
Fording: 1.22m (4ft)
Powerpack: Teledyne Continental AVDS 1790-2C V-12 diesel, developing 750bhp coupled to General Motors fully automatic transmission

General Dynamics M48A5 MBT

M48s were the only US MBTs to see action in Vietnam

The M48 MBT was developed from 1950, with first
production vehicles being completed in 1952.
Production continued until 1959, when the last of
over 11,700 vehicles was completed. The M48 series
was replaced in the United States Army by the M60
series which is a further development of the M48
including many improvements, such as a new turret,
105mm gun and diesel engine. The M48, M48C,
M48A1, M48A2 and M48A2C are all similar, being
armed with a 90mm gun and powered by a petrol
engine. The M48A3 is an earlier version, rebuilt, with
the most significant improvement being the
replacement of the petrol engine by a more fuel
efficient diesel engine. The M48A5 was the final

upgrade and included installation of a diesel engine and a 105mm rifled tank gun.

Standard equipment includes an NBC (Nuclear, Biological, Chemical) system, night vision equipment and provision for deep fording.

Many countries, including Germany, Greece, Israel, Spain, Taiwan and Turkey, have modified the M48 to meet local requirements.

Variants
M48 Armoured vehicle-launched bridge
M48 mine-clearer (Germany)

Specification

Crew: 4
Armament:
Main: 1 x 105mm gun
Co-axial: 1 x 7.62mm machine gun
Anti-aircraft: 2 x 7.62mm machine gun
Combat weight: 48,987kg (107,800lb)
Power-to-weight ratio: 15.89bhp/t
Length with gun: 9.306m (30.5ft)
Hull length: 6.419m (21.1ft)
Width: 3.631m (11.9ft)

Height: 3.086m (10.1ft)
Ground clearance: 0.419m (1.4ft)
Maximum road speed: 48.28km/h (30mph)
Range: 499km (309.4 miles)
Vertical obstacle: 0.915m (3ft)
Trench crossing: 2.59m (8.5ft)
Fording: 1.219m (4ft)
Powerpack: Teledyne Continental AVDS 1790-2D V-12 diesel, developing 750bhp coupled to General Motors CD-850-6A fully automatic transmission

M47 Medium Tank

Many NATO armies received M47s during the 1950s

The M47 medium tank was developed shortly after the end of the Second World War and over 8,600 were built. In United States Army service the M47 was soon replaced by the M48 and large numbers of M47s were then supplied to a number of countries' military aid programmes. In most countries the M47 is now in service, but in declining numbers.

Main armament comprises a 90 mm gun and, in addition to the 7.62mm co-axial machine gun, there is a 7.62mm machine gun mounted in the right side of the bow and a roof mounted 12.7mm machine gun. The petrol engine gives the M47 a very short operational range. As built, the M47 was not fitted with a computerised fire control system, an NBC (Nuclear, Biological, Chemical) system or passive night vision equipment.

The M47M, used in declining numbers by Iran, features automotive and fire control elements of the M60A1, but with the 90mm gun retained. The 7.62mm bow machine gun has been removed so that more 90mm ammunition can be carried.

Variants
M47M
M47 Armoured recovery vehicle

Specification

Crew: 5
Armament:
Main: 1 x 90mm gun
Co-axial: 1 x 7.62mm machine gun
Bow: 1 x 7.62mm machine gun
Anti-aircraft: 1 x 12.7mm machine gun
Combat weight: 46,170kg (101,574lb)
Power-to-weight ratio: 17.54bhp/t
Length with gun: 8.508m (28.2ft)
Hull length: 6.307m (21ft)

Width: 3.51m (11.5ft)
Height: 3.352m (11ft)
Ground clearance: 0.469m (1.54ft)
Maximum road speed: 48km/h (30mph)
Range: 130km (80 miles)
Vertical obstacle: 0.914m (3ft)
Trench crossing: 2.59m (8.5ft)
Fording: 1.219m (4ft)
Powerpack: Continental AV-1790-5B V-12 petrol, developing 750bhp coupled to Allison model CD-850-4 transmission

M4A3 Sherman Medium Tank

The M4 is another World War II veteran still in service

The M4 Sherman medium tank was developed in 1941 and, between 1942 and 1945, over 48,000 were built in many versions. It was phased out of US Army service in the 1950s and, by 1995, it remained in service with very few countries, although some versions have been used in the Yugoslav conflict.

The driver is seated at the left, with the bow machine gunner to his right, a turret in the centre and the engine at the rear. The Sherman is not fitted with an NBC (Nuclear, Biological, Chemical) system or night vision equipment. Some vehicles had a 76mm gun or a diesel engine. The British, however, developed the Sherman Firefly armed with a 17-pounder gun.

One of the largest users in the post Second World War period was Israel, which carried out many modifications including the M51 armed with a 105mm gun. Some of these have been sold to Chile. Israel still uses a number of Shermans in specialised roles including 155mm self-propelled artillery systems and a 160mm self-propelled mortar.

Variants
M7 105mm self-propelled gun
M10 and M36 tank destroyers
M32 and M74 Armoured recovery vehicles

Specification

Crew: 5
Armament:
Main: 1 x 75mm gun
bow: 1 x 7.62mm machine gun
Co-axial: 1 x 7.62mm machine gun
Anti-aircraft: 1 x 12.7mm machine gun
Combat weight: 31,070kg (68,354lb)
Power-to-weight ratio: 14.483hp/t
Length with gun: 5.905m (19.4ft)
Hull length: 5.905m 19.4ft)

Width: 2.667m (8.7ft)
Height: 2.743m (9ft)
Ground clearance: 0.434m (1.4ft)
Maximum road speed: 42km/h (26mph)
Range: 161km (99.8 miles)
Vertical obstacle: 0.609m (2ft)
Trench crossing: 2.26m (7.4ft)
Fording: 0.914m (3ft)
Powerpack: Ford GAA 8-cylinder petrol, developing 450hp coupled to manual transmission.

United Defense XM8 Armored Gun System

The futuristic XM-8 will equip US airborne forces

Following a competitive tender, in 1992, the now United Defense LP was awarded a contract by the United States Army for the development of the XM8 Armored Gun System as the replacement for the M551 light tank currently in use. By late 1994 a total of six prototypes had been built. It is anticipated that a total of 237 production vehicles will be built.

Main armament comprises a 105 mm rifled tank gun that fires standard NATO ammunition, fed from an automatic loader in the left side of the turret which holds 21 rounds of ready-use ammunition. It is fully stabilised and the computerised fire control systems give a high first round hit probability. The gunner has a day/thermal night sight with laser range-finder and the commander can also aim and fire the main armament under day and night conditions.

Standard equipment includes an NBC (Nuclear, Biological, Chemical) system, fire detection and suppression system, and the ability to be fitted with various additional armour packages for improved battlefield survivability. With the level III armour package, the combat weight is 22,680kg (50,009lb). The XM8 AGS has been designed to be air dropped from the C-130 Hercules transport aircraft.

Specification

Crew: 3

Armament:

Main: 1 x 105mm gun

Co-axial: 1 x 7.62mm machine gun

Anti-aircraft: 1 x 12.7mm machine gun

Combat weight: 17,463kg (38,418lb)

Power-to-weight ratio: 29hp/t

Length with gun: 9.19m (30.1ft)

Hull length: 6.1m (20ft)

Width: 2.69m (8.8ft)

Height: 2.55m (8.4ft)

Ground clearance: 0.41m (1.3ft)

Maximum road speed: 72.42km/h (45mph)

Range: 483km (299.4 miles)

Vertical obstacle: 0.812m (2.7ft)

Trench crossing: 2.133m (6.7ft)

Fording: 1.02m (3.3ft)

Powerpack: Detroit Diesel Model 6V-92TA, developing 550hp coupled to Martin Marietta HMPT-500-3EC automatic transmission

Cadillac Gage Stingray Light Tank

A Stingray light tank takes to the air as it demonstrates its astonishing agility

The Stingray light tank was developed specifically for the export market by the now Textron Marine & Land Systems, with the first prototype completed in 1984. So far, the only customer is Thailand, which purchased a total of 106 vehicles which were delivered between 1988 and 1990.

To reduce development and procurement costs, proven sub-systems have been used in the developing Stingray . The Royal Ordnance 105mm low recoil force gun, which is fitted with a muzzle brake, thermal sleeve and fume extractor, fires all standard natures of ammunition including APFSDS (Armour Piercing Fin Discarding Sabot).

Standard equipment includes a computerised fire control system. day/night sights for the commander and gunner, stabilised main armament, a computerised fire control system, a fire detection and supression system and an NBC (Nuclear, Biological, Chemical) system. Options include thermal sights, a land navigation system and different levels of protection. The Stingray II light tank, the prototype of which was completed in 1994/1995, has a number of improvements including a new armour package, an upgraded fire control system and thermal sight for the gunner, with a display for the commander.

Specification

Crew: 4
Armament:
Main: 1 x 105mm gun
Co-axial: 1 x 7.62mm machine gun
Anti-aircraft: 1 x 12.7mm machine gun
Combat weight: 21,205kg (46,651lb)
Power-to-weight ratio: 25.9hp/t
Length with gun: 9.30m (30.5ft)
Hull length: 6.448m (21.1ft)

Width: 2.71m (8.9ft)
Height: 2.55m (8.4ft)
Ground clearance: 0.46m (1.5ft)
Maximum road speed: 67km/h (41.5mph)
Range: 483km (299.5 miles)
Vertical obstacle: 0.76m (2.5ft)
Trench crossing: 2.13m (7ft)
Fording: 1.07m (3.5ft)
Powerpack: Detroit Diesel Model 8V-92TA ,developing 535hp coupled to Allison Transmission XTG-411-2A automatic transmission

M551 Sheridan Light Tank

The M551 did not live up to expectations in Vietnam

The M551 was developed as the replacement for the
M41 light tank and was accepted for service as the
M551 Armored Reconnaissance/Airborne Assault
Vehicle (AR/AAV), with a total of 1700 being built
between 1966 and 1970. By 1995, only one
operational battalion remained equipped with the
M551 and, in the future, the M551 will be replaced
by the M8 Armored Gun System (AGS).

The main armament of the M551 is a 152mm
weapon that can fire a conventional round with a
semi-combustible cartridge case or the Shillelagh anti-
tank guided missile. As built, the M551 had infra-red

night vision equipment, but more recently the driver has been provided with a image intensification night vision device, while the gunner has the Tank Thermal Sight (TTS) from the M60A3 MBT. The vehicle is fitted with a flotation screen which is normally carried, collapsed, around the top of the hull. When this is erected, the M551 is propelled in the water by its tracks at a maximum speed of 5.8km/h.

Large numbers of M551s are used at the United States Army National Training Center at Fort Irwin, but modified to resemble various vehicles of Russian design, such as the T-72 MBT.

Specification

Crew: 4
Armament:
Main: 1 x 152mm gun/launcher
Co-axial: 1 x 7.62mm machine gun
Anti-aircraft: 1 x 7.62mm machine gun
Combat weight: 15,830kg (34,826lb)
Power-to-weight ratio: 18.95bhp/t
Length with gun: 6.299m (20.7ft)
Hull length: 6.299m (20.7ft)

Width: 2.819m (9.2ft)
Height: 2.946m (9.7ft)
Ground clearance: 0.48m (1.ft)
Maximum road speed: 70km/h (43.4mph)
Range: 600km (372 miles)
Vertical obstacle: 0.838m (2.7ft)
Trench crossing: 2.54m (8.3ft)
Fording: amphibious
Powerpack: Detroit Diesel 6V-53T 6-cylinder turbo-charged diesel, developing 300bhp coupled to Allison XTG-250 automatic transmission

M41 Light Tank

The M41 light tank has been upgraded by the Brazilian and Danish armies

The M41 light tank was developed shortly after the end of the Second World War as the replacement for the M24 light tank. First production vehicles were completed in 1951. It was replaced in the United States Army by the M551 Sheridan light tank. Large numbers of M41s were supplied to overseas countries and these remain in service, although in declining numbers. Some countries have upgraded the M41 to extend their operational lives.

As built, the M41 was not fitted with any night vision equipment, a fire control system or an NBC (Nuclear, Biological, Chemical) system. Its main drawback was its petrol engine and short operational range. The Brazilian M41s have many improvements including a 90mm gun, additional armour protection and the replacement of the petrol engine by a more fuel efficient Scania DS-14A diesel, increasing its operational range.

The Danish M41s have been rebuilt to the M41 DK-1 configuration which not only includes a new Cummins VTA-903T diesel engine, increasing operational range to 750km, but also an NBC (Nuclear, Biological, Chemical) system, an all-electric gun control system, night vision devices and new 76mm ammunition.

Specification

Crew: 4
Armament:
Main: 1 x 76mm gun
Co-axial: 1 x 7.62mm machine gun
Anti-aircraft: 1 x 12.7mm machine gun
Combat weight: 23 495kg (51.7lb)
Power-to-weight ratio: 21.26bhp/t
Length with gun: 8.212m (26.9ft)
Hull length: 5.819m (19.1ft)
Width: 3.198m (10.5ft)

Height: 3.075m (10.1ft)
Ground clearance: 0.45m (1.5ft)
Maximum road speed: 72km/h (44.6mph)
Range: 161km (99.8 miles)
Vertical obstacle: 0.711m (2.3ft)
Trench crossing: 1.82m (6 ft)
Fording: 1.016m (3.3ft)
Powerpack: Continental AOS-895-3 6-cylinder petrol, developing 500bhp coupled to GMC Allison Division cross-drive Model CD-500-3 transmission

M-84A MBT

Production of M84 MBTs has just re-started in Serbia

The M-84 is the Russian T-72 MBT manufactured under licence, with many improvements and modifications, for the Yugoslav Army. Following trials, the M-84 was accepted for service, with first production vehicles being completed in 1984.

The main armament comprises a 125mm smooth bore gun which automatically loads the seperate ammunition, projectile and charge, into the gun. This has enabled the crew to be reduced to three men: commander, gunner and loader. The second production version has a number of improvements including additional armour protection and a more powerful engine. This is the model exported to Kuwait.

Standard equipment on the M-84A includes a computerised fire control system which includes a laser range-finder, day/night devices, an NBC (Nuclear, Biological, Chemical) system, a deep fording system and the ability to lay a smoke screen by injecting diesel fuel into the exhaust outlet. A dozer blade is mounted at the front of the hull. Mine-clearing equipment can also be fitted, if required.

Yugoslavia was developing another new MBT, the V 2001, but as far as is known, work on this stopped when the civil war broke out several years ago.

Variants
Armoured recovery vehicle
Command tank

Specification

Crew: 3
Armament:
Main: 1 x 125mm gun
Co-axial: 1 x 7.62mm machine gun
Anti-aircraft: 1 x 12.7mm machine gun
Combat weight: 42,000kg (92,400lb)
Power-to-weight ratio: 23.8hp/t
Length with gun: 9.53m (31.2ft)
Hull length: 6.86m (22 5ft)

Width: 3.59m (11.8ft)
Height: 2.19m (7.2ft)
Ground clearance: 0.5m (1.6ft)
Maximum road speed: 65km/h (40.3mph)
Range: 700km (434 miles)
Vertical obstacle: 0.85m (1.5ft)
Trench crossing: 2.8m (9.2ft)
Fording: 1.2m (3.9ft)
Powerpack: 12-cylinder multi-fuel diesel, developing 1000hp coupled to hydro-mechanical transmission.

ENGESA EE-9 Cascavel Armoured Car

The EE-9 is in widespread service in South America

The EE-9 Cascavel (6 x 6) armoured car was developed by the ENGESA company in 1970, and shares many common automotive components with the ENGESA EE-11 (6 x 6) armoured personnel carrier developed at the same time.

The first production EE-9s were completed in 1974 and were fitted with a turret armed with a 37 mm gun, and powered by a Mercedes-Benz diesel engine coupled to Clark manual tranmission. These were called the Mk II. The Mk III had the French 90 mm turret, while the Mk IV had the ENGESA ET-90 turret armed with ENGESA EC-90 gun, and were both powered by a Detroit Diesel Model 6V-53 developing 212 coupled to Allison MT-643 automatic transmission.

Later production models were the Mk V, Mk VI and Mk VII, with the latter being powered by a Mercedes-Benz OM 352A diesel, developing 190 hp coupled to Allison MT-643 transmission. Late production models also featured a central tyre pressure regulation system, a 24-V electrical system, a laser range-finder over a 90 mm gun, and a commander's cupola with an externally mounted 12.7 mm machine gun.

Specification

Crew: 3
Armament:
Main: 1 x 90mm gun
Co-axial: 1 x 7.62mm machine gun
Anti-aircraft: 1 x 12.7mm machine gun
Weight combat: 13,400kg (29,480lb)
Power-to-weight ratio: 15.82hp/t
Length with gun: 6.2m (20.3ft)
Hull length: 5.2m (17.1ft)
Width: 2.64m (8.7ft)

Height: 2.68m (8.8ft)
Ground clearance: 0.5m (1.6ft)
Maximum road speed: 100 km/h (62m/h)
Range: 880km (54.6m)
Vertical obstacle: 0.6m (1.2ft)
Trench: n/a
Fording: 1m (3.3ft)
Powerpack: Detroit Diesel Model 6V-53N 6-cylinder diesel, developing 212hp coupled to Allison Transmission MT-643 automatic transmission.

ENGESA EE-3 Jararaca Scout Car

The EE-3 scout car can carry MILAN anti-tank missiles

The EE-3 Jararaca (4 x 4) scout car was developed by ENGESA as a private venture, to compliment their EE-9 Cascavel (6 x 6) and EE-11 Urutu (6 x 6) armoured personnel carrier. The ENGESA company is no longer manufacturing armoured vehicles.

The basic EE-3 Jararaca was not amphibious. It was fitted with an externally mounted 12.7mm machine gun, but other armament options were also available including a 12.7mm machine gun that could be aimed and fired from within the vehicle, a turret with twin 7.62mm machine guns and a pintle-mounted Euromissile MILAN anti-tank guided missile launcher. The latter version is known to have been adopted by Cyprus. ENGESA developed turrets armed with 12.7mm/7.62mm machine guns and 20mm cannon/7.62mm machine gun, but these did not enter production for the EE-3.

Standard equipment includes a central tyre pressure regulation system which allows the driver to adjust the tyre pressure without leaving his seat. Optional equipment includes various types of passive night vision equipment, an NBC (Nuclear, Biological, Chemical) system and communications equipment. The NBC (Nuclear, Biological, Chemical) reconnaissance model has a raised superstructure.

Variants
Anti-tank with MILAN anti-tank guided missile
NBC (Nuclear, Biological, Chemical) reconnaissance

Specification

Crew: 3
Armament:
Main: 1 x 7.62mm machine gun
Weight combat: 5,800kg (12,760lb)
Power-to-weight ratio: 20.7hp/t
Hull length: 4.163m (13.7ft)
Width: 2.235m (7.3ft)
Height: 1.56m (5.1ft)
Ground clearance: 0.335m (1.1ft)

Maximum road speed:
100km/h (62m/h)
Range: 700km (434m)
Vertical obstacle: 0.40m (1.3ft)
Trench: n/a
Fording: 0.60m (2ft)
Powerpack: Mercedes-Benz OM 314A 4 cylinder diesel, developing 120hp coupled to Clark manual transmission.

Giat AMX-10RC Armoured Car

With a 105 mm gun, the AMX-10 can destroy MBTs

The AMX-10RC (6 x 6) armoured car was developed by the now Giat Industries as the replacement for the Panhard EBR (8 x 8) armoured car which has now been phased out of service with the French Army. Following extensive trials, first production vehicles were completed in 1980, with final production vehicles completed in late 1994.

The AMX-10RC shares a number of components with the tracked AMX-10P infantry combat vehicle. Standard equipment includes an NBC (Nuclear, Biological, Chemical) system, night vision equipment, and a hydro-pneumatic suspension system which allows the driver to adjust the ground clearance from 0.2 to 0.6m to suit the tactical situation. The AMX-10RC is fully amphibious, propelled in the water by two water-jets mounted, one either side, at the rear of the hull.

In the future, it is expected that the French Army AMX-10RC vehicles will be modified in a number of key areas including the installation of a 105mm rifled gun which fires standard NATO ammunition, by fitting a thermal camera and by mounting an anti-tank guided weapon decoy system, as well as by adding armour to hull and turret, a central tyre pressure regulation system and by modifying the transmission.

Variants
AMX-10RC driver training vehicle
AMX-10RC 105 TML (prototype)

Specification

Crew: 4
Armament:
Main: 1 x 105mm gun
Co-axial: 1 x 7.62mm machine gun
Weight combat: 15,880kg (34,936lb)
Power-to-weight ratio: 16.45hp/t
Length with gun: 9.15m (30ft)
Hull length: 6.357m (20.8ft)
Width: 2.95m (9.7ft)

Height: 2.66m (8.7ft)
Ground clearance: 0.35m (1.1ft)
Maximum road speed: 85km/h (52.7m/h)
Range: 1000km (620miles)
Vertical obstacle: 0.8m (2.6ft)
Trench: 1.65m (5.4ft)
Fording: amphibious
Powerpack: Hispano-Suiza HS 115 8-cylinder diesel, developing 260hp at 3000rpm coupled to pre-selective transmission.

Panhard ERC Sagaie 1 Armoured Car

The French army's ERC Sagaie 1s are fully amphibious

The Panhard ERC Sagaie 1 (6 x 6) armoured car was developed as a private venture from 1975 by Panhard, with the first prototypes being shown in 1977. It shares many common components with the Panhard VCR (6 x 6) armoured personnel carrier developed at the same time.

The standard ERC Sagaie 1 vehicle used by the French Army is fitted with the Giat Industries' TS 90 turret armed with a long-barrelled 90 mm gun. With preparation, this version is fully amphibious, propelled in the water by its wheels. Steering is power assisted on the front wheels and the centre wheels can be raised while travelling on roads. In addition to the wide range of turret options, the vehicle can also be

fitted with an NBC (Nuclear, Biological, Chemical)
system, various night observation devices, a land
navigation system, an air conditioning system, a
front-mounted winch and water-jets which give
maximum water speed of 9.5km/h.

Variants
ERC 90 F4 Sagaie TTB 190
ERC 90 F4 Sagaie 2
ERC 90 F1 Lynx
ERC 60-20 Serval
ERC 2 x 20mm SPAAG(self-propelled anti-aircraft gun)

Specification

Crew: 3
Armament:
Main: 1 x 90mm gun
Co-axial: 1 x 7.62mm machine
gun
Anti-aircraft: 1 x 7.62mm
machine gun
Weight combat: 81,00kg
(17,820lb)
Power-to-weight ratio:
19.13hp/t
Length with gun: 7.693m
(25.2ft)
Hull length: 5.098 m (16.7ft)

Width: 2.495m (8.2ft)
Height: 2.254m (7.4ft)
Ground clearance: 0.344m (1.1ft)
Maximum road speed:
95km/h (58.9m/h)
Range: 700 km (434m)
Vertical obstacle: 0.8m (2.6ft)
Trench: 1.1 m (3.6ft)
Fording: 1.2 m (3.9ft)
Powerpack: Peugeot V-6
petrol, developing 155hp
coupled to manual
transmission.

Panhard AML 90 Armoured Car

Over 40 armies have bought versions of the AML-90

The AML (4 x 4) armoured car was developed by Panhard for the French Army, with first production vehicles completed in 1962. The first two models were the AML 90, fitted with a two man 90 mm turret, and the AML 60-7, armed with 60 mm mortar and twin 7.62 mm machine guns.

The AML shares many common components with the Panhard M3 (4 x 4) armoured personnel carrier and total production of these vehicles, including those made under licence in South Africa (where it is known as the Eland), is over 6,000.

The vehicle has no NBC (Nuclear, Biological, Chemical) system, but optional equipment includes various night vision devices, a laser range-finder for a 90 mm gun, an air conditioning system and amphibious kit. Late production vehicles also have a more fuel efficient diesel engine.

Variants
AML HE 60-12 turret
AML HE 60-20 turret
AML HE 60-20 Serval turret
AML with twin 20 mm S 530 turret

Specification

Crew: 3
Armament:
Main: 1 x 90mm gun
Co-axial: 1 x 7.62mm machine gun
Combat weight: 5,500kg (12,100lb)
Power-to-weight ratio: 16.36hp/t
Length with gun: 5.11m (16.8ft)
Hull length: 3.79m (12.4ft)
Width: 1.97m (6.5ft)

Height: 2.07m (6.8ft)
Ground clearance: 0.33m (1.1ft)
Maximum road speed: 90km/h (55m/h)
Range: 600km (372m)
Vertical obstacle: 0.3m (1ft)
Trench: 0.8m (2.6ft)
Fording: 1.1m (3.6ft)
Powerpack: Panhard Model 4 HD 4-cylinder petrol, developing 90hp coupled to manual transmission

Panhard VBL Scout Car

VBLs are now serving with French units in the Balkans

The VBL (Vehicule Blinde Leger) (4 x 4) scout car
was developed by Panhard for the French Army, with
the first prototypes completed in 1983. Two years
later, it was accepted for service, by which time it was
already in production for Mexico. The French Army
uses two basic versions of the VBL: combat and
intelligence.

   The former has a three man crew and is armed with
a MILAN anti-tank guided missile and 7.62mm
machine gun, while the latter has a two man crew and
is armed with a 7.62mm or 12.7mm machine gun.
The vehicle is fully amphibious, propelled in the
water by a single propeller at a maximum speed of
5.4km/h.

Standard equipment on French Army vehicles includes an NBC (Nuclear, Biological, Chemical) system, run flat tyres and passive night vision equipment.

The standard version has a wheelbase of 2.45m, but there is also a version with a long wheelbase of 2.7m. This can be fitted with a wider range of weapon stations including turrets armed with 7.62mm or 12.7mm machine gun, as well as with radars and other surveillance devices.

Variants

There are well over 20 variants of the VBL offered by Panhard

Specification

Crew: 2 – 3
Ground clearance: 0.37m (1.2ft)
Armament:
Main: 1 x 7.62mm machine gun
1 x MILAN (anti-tank guided missile)
Maximum road speed: 95km/h (58.3m/h)
Range: 600km (372m)
Combat weight: 3,590kg (7,898lb)

Vertical obstacle: 0.25m (0.8ft)
Power-to-weight ratio: 26.76hp/t
Trench: 0.50m (1.6ft)
Fording: amphibious
Hull length: 3.87m (12.7ft)
Width: 2.02m (6.6ft)
Powerpack: Peugeot XD 3T4-cylinder diesel, developing 95hp coupled to ZF automatic transmission.
Height: 1.70m (5.6ft)

Spahpanzer Luchs Reconnaissance Vehicle

The Luchs has two drivers, one in front and one at the back to get out of trouble quickly

The Spahpanzer Luchs (8 x 8) amphibious reconnaissance vehicle was developed by Daimler Benz with Thyssen Henschel, building a total of 408 vehicles for the German Army between 1975 and 1978.

The vehicle is fully amphibious, propelled in the water by two propellers mounted at the rear of the hull, giving the vehicle a maximum water speed of 10km/h. An unusual feature of the Spahpanzer Luchs is that it has two drivers, one at the front and one at the rear, and can be driven at speeds of up to 90km/h in either direction. The two man power operated turret is armed with the same 20mm Rheinmetall cannon as is fitted to the Marder 1 infantry combat vehicle used by the German Army, with a 7.62mm machine gun mounted on the roof. The 20mm cannon is not stabilised. More recently, thermal night vision equipment has been fitted to the turret, when the vehicle is known as the Spahpanzer Luchs A2.

Standard equipment includes an NBC (Nuclear, Biological, Chemical) protection system, a preheater, power steering on all eight wheels and run flat tyres.

Specification

Crew: 4
Armament:
Main: 1 x 20mm cannon
Anti-aircraft: 1 x 7.62mm machine gun
Combat weight: 19,500kg (42,900lb)
Power-to-weight ratio: 20hp/t
Hull length: 7.743m (25.4ft)
Width: 2.98m (9.8ft)
Height: 2.905m (9.5ft)
Ground clearance: 0.44m (0.6ft)

Maximum road speed: 90km/h (55.8m/h)
Range: 730km (45.3miles)
Vertical obstacle: 0.60m (2ft)
Trench: 1.90m (6.2ft)
Fording: amphibious
Powerpack: Mercedes-Benz OM 403 A V-10 multi-fuel, developing 320hp (petrol), or 390hp (diesel), coupled to automatic transmission.

MaK MK 20 A1 Wiesel AWC

The Wiesel weapons carrier supports German parachute units

The Armoured Weapon Carrier Wiesel was designed for German airborne units by Porsche, with production being undertaken by MaK System Gesellschaft. A total of 345 vehicles were built between 1989 and 1992 in two versions: the two man MK 20 A1 armed with a 20mm cannon and the three man armed with a launcher for the Hughes TOW A2 anti-tank guided missile system.

 The vehicle has an all-welded steel hull, providing the occupants with protection from small arms fire. The driver is front right, with the engine to his left

and the weapons station to the rear. The vehicle has
no NBC (Nuclear, Biological, Chemical) system and
is not amphibious. A wide range of trial vehicles have
been built, including the Wiesel 2 Extended Base
Vehicle which has five road wheels either side and can
carry six men.

Early in 1995, the Wiesel chassis was selected as the
platform for the rapid deployment forces of German
Army's mobile air defence system and will be armed
with Stinger missiles.

Variants
MK 2O A1 (20 mm cannon)
TOW A2 (Hughes TOW anti-tank guided missile)

Specification

Crew: 2
Armament:
Main: 1 x 20mm cannon
Combat weight: 2,800kg
(6,160lb)
Power-to-weight ratio:
30.7hp/t
Length with gun: 3.545m
(11.6ft)
Hull length: 3.31m (11ft)
Width: 1.82m (6ft)
Height: 1.825m (6ft) .

Ground clearance: 0.302m (ft)
Maximum road speed:
75km/h (46m/h)
Range: 300km (186m)
Vertical obstacle: 0.4m (1.3ft)
Trench: 1.2m (4ft)
Fording: 0.5m (1.6ft)
Powerpack: VW 5-cylinder
diesel with exhaust turbo-
charger developing 86hp
coupled to automatic
transmission

FUG (or OT-65) Scout Car

Several former-Warsaw Pact armies operate the FUG

The FUG (4 x 4) amphibious scout car fulfils a similar role in the Hungarian Army to the Russian BRDM-1 (4 x 4) amphibious scout car. Following trials with prototype vehicles, it entered service with the Hungarian Army in 1964, and with the Czechoslovakian and Polish armies in 1966.

Armament consists of a pintle-mounted 7.62mm machine gun. Standard equipment includes a central tyre pressure regulation system that allows the driver to adjust the tyre pressure to suit the terrain being crossed, night vision equipment and an NBC (Nuclear, Biological, Chemical) system.

The FUG, which is known as the 'OT-65' in

Czechoslovakia, is fully amphibious, propelled in the water by two water-jets mounted at the rear of the hull, giving the vehicle a maximum water speed of 9 km/h. Like the Russian BRDM-1 and BRDM-2 vehicles, the FUG has a pair of powered belly-wheels on either side. When crossing rough terrain, these are lowered by the driver.

The Czech OT-65A is essentially the FUG/OT-65 fitted with the same turret, as is fitted to the OT-62B full tracked APC armed with a 7.62mm machine gun and with provision for an 82mm recoilless rifle.

Variants
Ambulance
NBC (Nuclear, Biological, Chemical) reconnaissance

Specification

Crew: 2 + 4
Armament:
Main: 1 x 7.62mm machine gun
Combat weight: 7,000kg (15,400lb)
Power-to-weight ratio: 15.87hp/t
Hull length: 5.79m (19ft)
Width: 2.50m (8.2ft)
Height: 1.91m (6.3ft)
Ground clearance: 0.34m (1.1ft)

Maximum road speed: 87km/h (53.9m/h)
Range: 600km (372m)
Vertical obstacle: 0.40m (1.3ft)
Trench: 1.20m (3.9ft)
Fording: amphibious
Powerpack: Csepel D.414.44 4-cylinder diesel, developing 100hp coupled to manual transmission.

RAMTA RAM V-1 Light Armoured Vehicle

Widely spaced wheels and the shaped hull protect the RAM's crew from mines

The RAM family of light (4 x 4) armoured vehicles was developed by RAMTA Structures and Systems, a division of Israel Aircraft Industries, from their earlier RBY Mk 1 light armoured reconnaissance vehicle. It is in service with a number of countries including Guatemala, Honduras, Israel and Lesotho.

The RAM family consists of two basic groups of vehicle, the RAM V-1 (long) which has an open roof, and the RAM V-2 (long) which has a closed roof. Both can be used for a wide range of roles. The hull of the vehicle is an all-welded steel armour construction with the wheels placed at the far ends of the vehicle to give maximum protection to the crew from mines. The engine is at the rear. The basic vehicle is used as a reconnaissance/infantry fighting vehicle, and is fitted with three 7.62mm machine guns or one 12.7mm and two 7.62mm machine guns. The RAM is not fitted with an NBC (Nuclear, Biological, Chemical) system and has no amphibious capability.

Standard equipment includes a front-mounted winch.

Variants
Anti-aircraft with 2 x 20mm cannon
Anti-tank with 106mm recoilless rifle
Anti-tank with TOW or MILAN anti-tank guided missile

Specification

Crew: 2 + 7
Armament:
Main: 3 x 7.62mm machine gun
Combat weight: 5,750kg (18,860lb)
Power-to-weight ratio: 22.95hp/t
Hull length: 5.52m (18.1ft)
Width: 2.03m (6.7ft)
Height: 1.72m (5.6ft)
Ground clearance: 0.575m (1.9ft)

Maximum road speed: 96km/h (60m/h)
Range: 800km (496m)
Vertical obstacle: 0.8m (2.6ft)
Trench: nil
Fording: 0.75m (2.46ft)
Powerpack: Deutz 6-cylinder diesel, developing 132hp coupled to Allison automatic transmission.

B1 Centauro Tank Destroyer

The Centauro tank destroyer first saw action in Somalia

The B1 Centauro (8 x 8) tank destroyer has been
developed by a consortium consisting of two
companies, IVECO and OTOBREDA (previously
OTO Melara), with the former being responsible for
the complete powerpack, suspension system, chassis and
final integration and OTOBREDA for the complete
turret and weapon system. Following trials with
prototypes, the Italian Army placed an order for 400
vehicles, and the first of these was completed in 1991.

Main armament comprises a 105mm rifled gun fitted
with a muzzle brake, thermal sleeve, fume extractor and
muzzle reference system which fires standard NATO
ammunition including APFSDS (armour-piercing, fin-
discarding sabot) types. The 105mm gun is fully

stabilised in elevation and traverse, and the computerised fire control system includes stabilised day/night sights for commander and gunner.

Standard equipment includes a central tyre pressure regulation system, power steering on the front four wheels, a winch, a fire detection/suppression system and NBC (Nuclear, Biological, Chemical) system.

For operations in Somalia some vehicles were fitted with explosive reactive armour, as developed by Royal Ordnance of the UK. For trials, a prototype of the B1 Centauro is being converted into an armoured personnel carrier. A test bed for a 155mm (8 x 8) self-propelled artillery system has also been built.

Specification

Crew: 4
Armament:
Main: 1 x 105mm gun
Co-axial: 1 x 7.62mm machine gun
Anti-aircraft: 1 x 7.62mm machine gun
Combat weight: 24,000kg (52,800lb)
Power-to-weight ratio: 21.66hp/t
Length with gun: 8.555m (28.1ft)

Hull length: 7.4m (24.3ft)
Width: 3.05m (10ft)
Height: 2.72m (9ft)
Ground clearance: 0.417m (1.4ft)
Maximum road speed: 100km/h (62m/h)
Range: 800km (496miles)
Fording: 1.5m (5ft)
Powerpack: IVECO V-6 MTCA diesel, developing 520hp coupled to ZF 5 HP 1500 automatic transmission.

129

Melara Type 6616 Armoured Car

The Type 6616 is now in service with Italy and Peru

The Type 6616 armoured car was developed as a private venture by two companies, FIAT (now IVECO) and OTO Melara (now OTOBREDA), with the former responsible for the hull and automotive aspects, and the latter for the turret and weapon system. The first prototype was completed in 1972, with first production vehicles completed shortly afterwards.

The Type 6616 armoured car shares many common automotive components with the Type 6614 armoured personnel carrier, also developed by FIAT and OTO Melara.

The Type 6616 is fitted with a two man power-operated turret armed with Rheinmetall 20mm cannon and a 7.62mm co-axial machine gun. The vehicle is fully amphibious, propelled in the water by by its wheels at a maximum speed of 5km/h.

Standard equipment includes powered steering, run flat tyres and electric bilge pumps. As built, it was not fitted with a passsive night vision equipment, an NBC (Nuclear, Biological, Chemical) system or winch. These were optional extras.

For trials purposes, the Type 6616 was fitted with a two man turret armed with a Cockerill 90 mm gun and 7.62mm machine gun, and two man turret with 60mm High Velocity Gun System and 7.62mm machine gun.

Specification

Crew: 4
Armament:
Main: 1 x 20mm cannon
Co-axial: 1 x 7.62mm machine gun
Combat weight: 8,000kg (17,600lb)
Power-to-weight ratio: 20.20hp/t
Hull length: 5.37m (17.6ft)
Width: 2.50m (8.2ft)
Height: 2.035m (6.7ft)

Ground clearance: 0.485m (1.6ft)
Maximum road speed: 100km/h (62m/h)
Range: 700km (434m)
Vertical obstacle: 0.42m (1.4ft)
Trench: nil
Fording: amphibious
Powerpack: FIAT model 8062.24 supercharged diesel, developing 160hp coupled to manual transmission.

131

Type 87 Reconnaissance Vehicle

The Type 87 reconnaissance vehicle is unusual in having a five-man crew

The Type 87 (6 x 6) reconnaissance and patrol vehicle was developed by Komatsu Limited for the Japanese Ground Self Defence Force and uses many automotive components of the Type 82 (6 x 6) command and communications.

The vehicle is an all-welded steel armour construction which provides protection from small arms fire and shell splinters. The layout of the Type 87 reconnaissance vehicle is unusual, with the driver seated at the front left, the radio operator to his right, a turret in the centre, and a powerpack at the rear, on the right, with the rear facing observer on the left. The two man power-operated turret was designed and built by Mitsubishi Heavy Industries to have the gunner on the left and commander on the right. The armament comprises a 25mm Oerlikon-Contraves 25mm KBA cannon with a 7.62mm machine gun mounted co-axially with the main armament. A bank of three electrically operated smoke grenade dischargers is mounted either side of the turret firing forwards.

Standard equipment includes power assisted steering and passive night vision equipment. It is not amphibious.

Specification

Crew: 5
Armament:
Main: 1 x 25mm cannon
Co-axial: 1 x 7.62mm machine gun
Combat weight: 15,000kg (49,200lb)
Power-to-weight ratio: 20.33hp/t
Hull length: 5.99m (19.6ft)
Width: 2.48m (8.1ft)
Height: 2.8m (9.1ft)

Ground clearance: 0.45m (1.5ft)
Maximum road speed: 100km/h (62m/h)
Range: 500km (310m)
Vertical obstacle: 0.6m (2ft)
Trench: 1.5m (4.9ft)
Fording: 1m (3.3ft)
Powerpack: Isuzu 10PBI 10-cylinder water cooled diesel, developing 305hp coupled to automatic transmission.

133

Mitsubishi Type 82 Command Vehicle

The Japanese Type 82 serves as a mobile command and control post

The Type 82 (6 x 6) command and communications vehicle was developed by Mitsubishi Heavy Industries for the Japanese Ground Self Defence Force and uses many automotive components of the Type 87 (6 x 6) reconnaissance and patrol vehicle. The first Type 82 prototypes were completed in 1980 and it is expected that a total of 250 vehicles will be procured under current plans.

The vehicle is of all-welded steel armour construction which provides protection from small arms fire and shell splinters. Firing ports and vision devices are provided for the crew. The layout of the Type 82 command and communications vehicle is unusual, with the driver and one crew member at the front, powerpack in the centre and the remainder of the crew in the raised compartment at the rear.

The 7.62 mm machine gun is normally pintle-mounted at the front of the hull, on the right, with the 12.7 mm machine gun provided with a shield, mounted on the roof.

Standard equipment includes power assisted steering and passive night vision equipment. It is not amphibious.

Specification

Crew: 8
Armament:
Main: 1 x 12.7mm machine gun
Secondary: 1 x 7.62mm machine gun
Combat weight: 13,500kg (29,700lb)
Power-to-weight ratio: 22.59hp/t
Length: 5.72m (18.8ft)
Width: 2.48m (8.1ft)
Height: 2.37m (7.8ft)

Ground clearance: 0.45m (1.5ft)
Maximum road speed: 100km/h (62m/h)
Range: 500km (186 miles)
Vertical obstacle: 0.6m (2ft)
Trench: 1.5m (5ft)
Fording: 1m (3.3ft)
Powerpack: Isuzu 10PBI 10-cylinder water-cooled diesel, developing 305hp coupled to automatic transmission.

BRDM-2 Armoured Car

The BRDM-2 was exported to almost every Soviet ally in Europe, the Middle East and Africa

The BRDM-2 (4 X 4) was developed in the early 1960s as the replacement for the BRDM-1 armoured car. The manually-operated turret mounted in the centre of the hull top is the same as that fitted to the BTR-60PB and the OT-64 armoured personnel carriers. It has a 14.5 mm heavy machine gun and a co-axial 7.62 mm weapon. It is unusual in having no roof hatch.

The BRDM-2 is fully amphibious, being propelled in the water by a single water jet mounted on the rear of the hull. Before entering the water, a trim vane is erected at the front of the hull.

Stardard equipment includes an NBC (Nuclear,

Biological, Chemical) defence system, night vision devices and a central tyre pressure regulation system. Mounted either side of the hull between the front and rear wheels are two small powered belly wheels which are lowered to the ground when crossing trenches and other obstacles.

Variants
BRDM-2-RKhb NBC reconnaissance
BRDM-2U command
BRDM-2 with Sagger anti-tank guided missile
BRDM-2 with Swatter anti-tank guided missile
BRDM-2 with Spandrel anti-tank guided missile
SA-9 Gaskin surface-to-air missile

Specification

Crew: 4
Armament:
Main: 1 x 14.5mm machine gun
Co-axial: 1 x 7.62mm machine gun
Combat Weight: 7,000kg (15,400lbs)
Power-to-weight ratio: 20hp/t
Hull length: 5.75m (18.86ft)
Width: 2.35m (7.71ft)
Height: 2.31m (7.57ft)

Ground clearance: 0.43m (1.41ft)
Maximum road speed: 100km/h (62mph)
Range: 750km (465 miles)
Vertical obstacle: 0.4m (1.31ft)
Trench crossing: 1.25m (4.10ft)
Fording: amphibious
Powerpack: GAZ-41 V-8 petrol engine developing 140hp coupled to manual transmission

BRDM-1 Scout Car

BRDM-1s soldier on in Cuba and in several African armies

The BRDM-1 (4 x 4) amphibious scout car was developed in the 1950s and built in large numbers by the Molotov GAZ plant for both home and export models. In the Russian Army it was replaced by the BRDM-2 (4 x 4) armoured car.

Armament normally comprises a pintle-mounted 7.62mm machine gun on the forward part of the turret roof, although some vehicles are fitted with a 12.7mm machine gun at the front and a 7.62mm machine gun at the rear. The BRDM-1 is fully amphibious, propelled in the water by a single water-jet mounted at the rear of the hull. The vehicle is not fitted with an NBC (Nuclear, Biological, Chemical) system and, as built, was not fitted with any night vision devices.

A central tyre pressure regulation system is fitted as standard, allowing the driver to adjust the tyre pressure to suit the type of ground being crossed. Mounted either side of the hull, between the front and rear wheels, are two small-powered belly-wheels which are lowered to the ground to enable trenches and other obstacles to be crossed.

Variants

BRDM-1-RKhb NBC (Nuclear, Biological, Chemical) reconnaissance
BRDM-1U command
BRDM-1 with Sagger anti-tank guided missile
BRDM-1 with Swatter anti-tank guided missile
BRDM-1 with Snapper anti-tank guided missile

Specification

Crew: 5
Armament:
Main: 1 x 7.62mm machine gun
Combat weight: 5,600kg (12,320lb)
Power-to-weight ratio: 16.07hp/t
Hull length: 5.7m (18.7ft)
Width: 2.25m (7.4ft)
Height: 1.90m (6.2ft)
Ground clearance: 0.315m (1.0ft)

Maximum road speed: 80km/h (49.6m/h)
Range: 500km (310m)
Vertical obstacle: 0.4m (0.2ft)
Trench: 1.22m (4ft)
Fording: amphibious
Powerpack: GAZ-40P 6-cylinder petrol, developing 90hp coupled to manual transmission.

LIW/Reumech OMC Rooikat Armoured Car

The Rooikat builds on combat experience in Namibia

The Rooikat (8 x 8) armoured car was developed for the South African Armoured Corps from 1976 and, following trials with prototype vehicles, was accepted for service, with first production vehicles completed in 1989. Reumech OMC is the prime contractor, responsible for the chassis and systems integration, while LIW, part of Denel, is responsible for the complete turret and associated 76mm rifled weapon system.

Standard equipment includes day/night sights, a computerised fire control system, a fire detection and suppression system and power-assisted steering. Optional equipment includes a chemical and biological overpressure collective system which is integrated with an air conditioning system.

Of the variants listed below, only the Rooikat 105mm

is being currently marketed. This is armed with a
105mm gun which fires standard NATO ammunition
and has larger tyres. If required, a central tyre pressure
regulation system can be fitted allowing the driver to
adjust the tyre pressure to suit the terrain being crossed.

Variants
Rooikat 35mm reconnaissance
Rooikat 35mm/anti-tank guided missile
Rooikat 105mm
Rooikat 2 x 35mm SPAAG (self-propelled anti-
aircraft gun)
Rooikat SAM (surface-to-air missile) system

Specification

Crew: 4
Armament:
Main: 1 x 76mm gun
Co-axial: 1 x 7.62mm machine gun
Anti-aircraft: 1 x 7.62mm machine gun
Combat weight: 28,000kg (61,600lb)
Power-to-weight ratio: 20.11hp/t
Length with gun: 8.2m (26.9ft)

Hull length: 7.09m (23.3ft)
Width: 2.90m (9.5ft)
Height: 2.80m (9.2ft)
Ground clearance: 0.4m (1.3ft)
Maximum road speed: 120km/h (74m/h)
Range: 1000km (620miles)
Vertical obstacle: 1m (3.3ft)
Trench: 2m (7.6ft)
Fording: 1.5m (4.92ft)
Powerpack: V-10 diesel, developing 563hp coupled to automatic transmission.

SANTA BARBARA VEC Scout Vehicle

The fully amphibious VEC scout vehicle is only used by the Spanish army

The VEC (6 x 6) cavalry scout vehicle was developed by Pegaso for the Spanish Army and shares many common automotive components with the BMR-600 (6 x 6) infantry fighting vehicle. First prototypes of the VEC were completed in 1977 and the vehicle is now in service with the Spanish Army.

The standard production VEC is fitted with a two man power operated turrets armed with a 25 mm McDonnell Douglas Helicopters Chain Gun and a 7.62 mm co-axial machine gun.

The Spanish Army also has a small number of vehicles fitted with the complete turret of the AML 90 armoured car, armed with a 90mm gun and 7.62mm co-axial machine gun.

The BMR-600 is fully amphibious, propelled in the water by its wheels, although, as an option, two water-jets can be mounted, on either side of the hull rear, giving the vehicle a maximum water speed of 9km/h.

Standard equipment includes hydro pneumatic suspension, powered steering on front and rear wheels, an NBC (Nuclear, Biological, Chemical) system, night vision equipment and a winch.

Specification

Crew: 3 + 2
Armament:
Main: 1 x 25mm cannon
Co-axial: 1 x 7.62mm machine gun
Combat weight: 13,750kg (45,100lb)
Power-to-weight ratio: 22.25hp/t
Hull length: 6.10m (20ft)
Width: 2.5m (8.2ft)
Height: 2m (6.6ft)

Ground clearance: 0.4m (1.3ft)
Maximum road speed: 103km/h (63.8m/h)
Range: 800km (496miles)
Vertical obstacle: 0.6m (2ft)
Trench: 1.5m (4.9ft)
Fording: amphibious
Powerpack: Pegaso 9157/8 6-cylinder diesel, developing 310hp coupled to ZF 6 HP 500 automatic transmission.

Alvis Saladin Armoured Car

No longer in British service, the Saladin is still used by several Commonwealth armies

The Alvis Saladin (6 x 6) armoured car was developed after the end of the Second World War, with the first prototypes built in 1953 and production carried out at Coventry between 1958 and 1972. The Saladin shares many common components with the Alvis Saracen (6 x 6) armoured personnel carrier. The main role of the Saladin is reconnaissance, but in the British Army it was replaced by the 76 mm armed Alvis Scorpion

Combat Vehicle Reconnaissance (Tracked).

Steering is power-assisted on the front four wheels and, as built, it was not fitted with an an NBC (Nuclear, Biological, Chemical) system or passive night vision equipment. More recently Alvis and A. F. Budge have developed an upgrade package for the Saladin to extend its operational life into the 21st Century. The modifications include the replacement of the petrol engine by a more fuel efficient Perkins 180 MTi diesel, developing 180hp coupled to a new automatic transmission. Indonesia is the first customer for this upgrade package.

Specification

Crew: 3
Armament:
Main: 1 x 76mm gun
Co-axial: 1 x 7.62mm machine gun
Anti-aircraft: 1 x 7.62mm machine gun
Combat weight: 11,590kg (25,498lb)
Power-to-weight ratio: 14.66hp/t
Length with gun: 5.284m (17.3ft)
Hull length: 4.93m (16 2ft)

Width: 2.54m (8.3ft)
Height: 2.39m (7.8ft)
Ground clearance: 0.426m (1.4ft)
Maximum road speed: 72km/h (44.m/h)
Range: 400km (247miles)
Vertical obstacle: 0.46m (1.5ft)
Trench: 1.52m (5ft)
Fording: 1.07m (3.5ft)
Powerpack: Rolls-Royce B80 petrol, developing 170hp coupled to preselector 5-speed transmission.

Shorts Shorland S52 Armoured Patrol Car

The Shorland S52 is based on a Land Rover chassis

The Shorland (4 x 4) armoured patrol car was developed in 1965 for the Royal Ulster Constabulary. By early 1995, over 1,000 Shorland vehicles had been built, with the latest generation being the 5-series based on the Land Rover Defender 110 inch chassis, with the option of a petrol or diesel engine.

Today there are four vehicles in the Shorland family: the S52 armoured patrol car, the S53 air defence vehicle, the S54 anti-hijack vehicle and the S55 armoured personnel carrier. The basic S52 Shorland is fitted with a manually operated one man turret ,armed with a 7.62mm machine gun, with the option of mounting two banks of four electrically operated smoke grenade dischargers on either side of the turret.

Standard equipment includes power steering, bullet-proof windows, extraction fans, an air conditioning system and seat belts, while optional equipment consists of drop-down visors with vision blocks in place of the bullet-resistant windscreen, as well as run flat tyres, a loud hailer and automatic fire protection.

Variants
S53 mobile air defence vehicle with SAMs (surface-to-air missiles)
S54 anti-hijack vehicle
S55 armoured personnel carrier

Specification

Crew: 3
Armament:
Main: 1 x 7.62mm machine gun
Combat weight: 3,600kg (7,920lb)
Power-to-weight ratio:
37.8bhp/t (petrol)
30.5bhp/t (diesel)
Hull length: 4.49m (14.7ft)
Width: 1.80m (5.9ft)
Height: 1.80m (5.9ft)
Ground clearance: 0.324m (1.1ft)

Maximum road speed:
120km/h (74m/h)
Range: 650km (404miles)
Vertical obstacle: 0.23m (0.7ft)
Trench: nil
Fording: nil
Powerpack: Rover 3.5 litre V-8 petrol, developing 134bhp, or 2.5 litre Land Rover TDi diesel, developing 107bhp coupled to manual transmission.

147

Daimler Ferret Mk 2/3 Scout Car

Over twenty armies still employ the British Ferret armoured scout car

The Ferret family of 4 x 4 scout cars was developed by the Daimler company from 1948, and a total of 4409 vehicles were built for the home and export markets between 1952 and 1971. It has only recently been phased out of service with the British Army.

The driver is at the front, a commander in the centre and the the powerpack at the rear. The one man manually operated turret is armed with a 7.62mm machine gun.

The Ferret series of vehicles were not provided with

an NBC (Nuclear, Biological, Chemical) system or passive night vision equipment, although some countries have fitted the latter.

Variants
Mk 1, open top with 7.62mm machine gun
Mk 1/2, covered roof with 7.62mm machine gun
Mk 2, turret armed with 7.62mm machine gun
Mk 2/3, turret armed with 7.62mm machine gun
Mk 2/6, turret armed with 7.62mm machine gun and Vigilant anti-tank guided missile
Mk 3, turret armed with 7.62mm machine gun
Mk 4, earlier model rebuilt with larger wheels
Diesel: Malaysian vehicles have been upgraded and fitted with a more fuel efficient Perkins diesel engine

Specification

Crew: 2
Armament:
Main: 1 x 7.62mm machine gun
Combat weight: 4,400kg (9,680lb)
Power-to-weight ratio: 29.35bhp/t
Hull length: 3.835m (12.6ft)
Width: 1.905m (6.4ft)
Height: 1.906m (6.2ft)
Ground clearance: 0.33m (1.1ft)

Maximum road speed: 93km/h (57.7m/h)
Range: 300km (186miles)
Vertical obstacle: 0.406m (1.3ft)
Trench: 1.22m (4ft)
Fording: 0.914m (3ft)
Powerpack: Rolls-Royce B60 Mk 6A 6-cylinder petrol, developing 129bhp coupled to pre-selective 5-speed transmission.

Cadillac Gage Scout

Egypt and Indonesia are the first customers for the Scout

The Scout (4 x 4) reconnaissance vehicle was developed as a private venture by the former Cadillac Gage Textron company, now the Textron Marine & Land Systems Division of Textron Incorporated. The first prototype was completed in 1977, with Indonesia placing an order for the vehicle in 1983 and Egypt following in 1986.

The Scout has the driver front left, with the powerpack to his right. At the rear is space for one or two men. Typical weapons fit are a Cadillac Gage twin / combination machine gun (1m) turret, armed with twin 7.62mm or 12.7mm machine guns or a combination of 7.62mm and 12.7mm machine guns.

Standard equipment includes power assisted steering. As built, it was not fitted with an NBC (Nuclear, Biological, Chemical) system or night vision equipment.

It is not amphibious.

A wide range of optional equipment could be fitted including a siren/public address system, various radio installations, water/petrol cans for extended operational range, as well as weapon stowage, a slave cable, an 15m auxiliary cable, a camouflage net, passive night vision equipment.

Variants
40mm/12.7mm turret
Twin 7.62mm turret (manual)
Twin 12.7mm turret (manual)
7.62mm/12.7mm turret (manual)
Command/pod
Anti-tank

Specification

Crew: 1 + 1
Armament:
Main: 2 x 7.62mm machine gun
Combat weight: 7,240kg (15,928lb)
Power-to-weight ratio: 20.58hp/t
Hull length: 5.003m (16.4ft)
Width: 2.057m (6.7ft)
Height: 2.159m (7.1ft)

Maximum road speed: 96km/h (59.5m/h)
Range: 1,287km (798 miles)
Vertical obstacle: 0.609m (2ft)
Trench: nil
Fording: 1.68m (5.5ft)
Powerpack: Cummins V-6 diesel, developing 149hp coupled to Allison automatic transmission.

M8 Armoured Car

The veteran M8 survives in Africa and Central America

The M8 (6 x 6) armoured car was developed in the Second World War for the US Army and a total of 8,523 were built by the Ford Motor Company between 1943 and 1945. It has long been phased out of service with the United States Army, but it is still found in service, often with modifications, in some parts of the world.

The hull and turret is of all steel construction, with the driver and co-driver at the front, an open-topped, manually operated turret in the centre and powerpack at the rear. Main armament comprises a 37mm gun with an elevation of +20 degrees and a depression of -10 degrees, with turret traverse a full 360 degrees. A 7.62mm machine gun is mounted co-axially to the left, with a 12.7mm machine gun on a pintle or ring mount. The vehicle is not provided with an NBC (Nuclear, Biological, Chemical) system or passive night vision equipment. NAPCO have fitted some M8s with a diesel, TOW anti-tank guided missile launcher and replaced 37mm gun by 12.7mm machine gun.

Variants
M20 armoured utility car

Specification

Crew: 4
Armament:
Main: 1 x 37mm gun
Co-axial: 1 x 7.62mm machine gun
Anti-aircraft: 1 x 12.7mm machine gun
Combat weight: 7,892kg (17,362.4lb)
Power-to-weight ratio: 13.93hp/t
Hull length: 5.003m (16.4ft)
Width: 2.54m (8.33ft)

Height: 2.247m (7.4ft)
Ground clearance: 0.29m (1ft)
Maximum road speed: 90km/h (55.8m/h)
Range: 560km (347 miles)
Vertical obstacle: 0.304m (1.2ft)
Trench: n/ap
Fording: 0.609m (2ft)
Powerpack: Hercules JXD 6-cylinder petrol, developing 110hp at 3000rpm coupled to manual transmission.

4KA 7FA G 127 APC

The 4KA can also be fitted with a 90 mm gun turret

The Steyr-Daimler-Puch 4K 7FA G 127 armoured personnel carrier is a further development of the older 4K 4FA series of vehicle, of which 445 were built for the Austrian Army by 1969. In Austrian Army service these are armed with a 12.7mm machine gun, although the 4K 4FA-G2 has a one man turret armed with a 20mm Oerlikon Contraves cannon.

Main improvements over the earlier 4K 4FA include increase armour protection over the frontal arc, and the complete engine and transmission of the Steyr-Daimler-Puch SK 105 tank destroyer/light tank. The standard model of the 4K 7FA G 127 is armed with a 12.7mm machine gun which is provided with a shield. In addition, 7.62mm machine guns can be mounted externally over the rear of the troop compartment. A wide range of other turrets is available including a two man turret armed with 90mm gun, a two man turret with 30mm cannon and various anti-aircraft weapons.

Standard equipment includes a heater and ventilating system. Optional equipment includes an NBC (Nuclear, Biological, Chemical) system, a fire detection/suppression system, an air conditioning system and passive night vision equipment.

Variants
Armoured ambulance
Command post vehicle
81mm mortar carrier

Specification

Crew: 2 + 8
Armament: 1 x 12.7mm machine gun
Combat weight: 14,800kg (32,560lb)
Power-to-weight ratio: 21.62hp/t
Hull length: 5.87m (19.3ft)
Width: 2.5m (8.2ft)
Height: 1.611m (5.2ft)
Ground clearance: 0.42m (1.4ft)

Maximum road speed: 70km/h (43mph)
Range: 520km (322 miles)
Vertical obstacle: 0.8m (2.6ft)
Trench: 2.1m (6.9ft)
Fording: 1.0m (3.3ft)
Powerpack: Steyr 7FA 6-cylinder turbocharged diesel developing 320hp coupled to ZF 6-S80 manual transmission

Steyr-Daimler-Puch Pandur APC

The first Pandurs are now entering service with Austria

The Pandur (6 x 6) armoured personnel carrier has been developed by the company Steyr-Daimler-Puch as a private venture and was shown for the first time in 1985. In early 1994 the Austrian Army placed a first production order for the Pandur, with first production vehicles completed in early 1995. They are to be used by units of the Austrian Army operating under United Nations command.

The Pandur can be fitted with a wide variety of armament installations ranging from a pintle-mounted 7.62mm or 12.7mm machine gun up to a two man operated turret armed with a 90mm gun and fitted with day/night sights and a computerised fire control system.

Standard equipment includes a central tyre pressure regulation system allowing the driver to adjust the ground pressure to suit the ground being crossed, as well as power steering, run flat tyres, firing ports/vision devices and a fire detection/extinguishing system for the engine compartment.

Variants

APC 127 (12.7mm machine gun)
ARFSV (90mm)
ARSV 30 (30mm)
ARV (Armoured Recovery Vehicle) Ambulance
Anti-aircraft (surface-to-air missile)
Anti-tank (HOT anti-tank guided missile)
Command post
81mm mortar

Specification

Crew: 2 + 8
Armament: 1 x 12.7mm machine gun
Combat weight: 13,000kg (42,640lb)
Power-to-weight ratio: 26.6hp/t
Hull length: 5.697m (18.7ft)
Width: 2.5m (8.2ft)
Height: 1.82m (6ft)
Ground clearance: 0.43m (1.4ft)
Maximum road speed: 100km/h (62mph)
Range: 600km (372 miles)
Vertical obstacle: 0.5m (1.6ft)
Trench: 1.6m (5.2ft)
Fording: 1.2m (4ft)
Powerpack: Steyr-Daimler-Puch WD 612.95 6-cylinder diesel developing 260hp coupled to Allison Transmission MT-653 DR automatic transmission

SIBMAS APC

The Belgian Sibmas is only in service with Malaysia

The SIBMAS (6 x 6) armoured personnel carrier was developed from 1975 by B N Constructions Ferroviaires et Metalliques as a private venture. The first prototype was completed in 1976. The design of the SIBMAS uses standard commercial components wherever possible.

The only customer for the SIBMAS was Malaysia. A total of 186 vehicles was purchased in 1981; the order compromising 162 AFSV 90 (Armoured Fire Support Vehicle 90 mm) variants and 24 ARVs (Armoured Recovery Vehicles). These were delivered between 1983 and 1986. The SIBMAS is no longer in production and is no longer being marketed.

The AFSV 90 is fitted with a two man turret armed with a 90 mm gun and a co-axial 7.62 mm machine gun. Smoke dischargers are fitted on the side of the turret. The ARV is fitted with a winch and crane instead of the turret. Both versions are fully amphibious, being propelled in the water by the wheels at a maximum speed of 4 km/h, or by two propellers in the rear at up to 11 km/h. Standard equipment includes run-flat tyres and power steering.

Variants
AFSV 90
ARV

Specification

Crew: 3 + 11
Armament:
Main: 1 x 90mm gun
Co-axial: 1 x 7.62mm machine gun
Anti-aircraft: 1 x 7.62mm machine gun
Combat weight: 14,500kg
Power-to-weight ratio: 20hp/t
Hull length: 7.32m (24.01ft)
Width: 2.5m (8.20ft)
Height: 2.7m (8.85ft)

Ground clearance: 0.4m (1.31ft)
Maximum road speed: 100km/h (62.1mph)
Range: 1000km (621miles)
Vertical obstacle: 2.29m
Trench crossing: 4.92m
Fording: amphibious
Powerpack: MAN D 2566 mk 6-cylinder diesel developing 320hp coupled to ZF automatic transmission

ENGESA EE-11 Mk VII Urutu APC

The amphibious Urutu is in use throughout South America

The EE-11 Urutu (6 x 6) armoured personnel carrier was developed by the ENGESA company in 1970, and shares many common automotive components with the ENGESA EE-9 (6 x 6) armoured car developed at the same time. First production EE-11s were completed in 1974 and, by the time production was completed, no less than seven different models had been built and designated Mk I through to VII.

A wide range of weapons was offered, ranging from pintle-mounted 7.62mm and 12.7mm machine guns up to a one man 20mm turret and a two man 90mm turret, which was also fitted to the EE-9 Cascavel armoured car. The EE-11 Urutu is fully amphibious, propelled in the water by two propellers mounted at the rear of the hull.

A wide range of optional equipment was offered, including an NBC (Nuclear, Biological, Chemical) system, and a fire detection and suppression system. Late production vehicles have a central tyre pressure regulation system.

Variants

Armoured Fire Support Vehicle with a 90mm turret
Ambulance
Cargo carrier
Command post vehicle

Specification

Crew: 1 + 12
Armament: 1 x 12.7mm machine gun
Combat weight: 14,000kg (30,800lb)
Power-to-weight ratio: 18.6hp/t
Hull length: 6.1m (20.1ft)
Width: 2.65m (8.7ft)
Height: 2.90m (9.5ft)
Ground clearance: 0.38m (1.3ft)
Maximum road speed:

105km/h (65.1mph)
Range: 850km (527 miles)
Vertical obstacle: 0.6m (1.96ft)
Trench: n/a
Fording: amphibious
Powerpack: Detroit Diesel Model 6V-53T 6-cylinder diesel developing 260hp coupled to Allison Transmission MT-643 automatic transmission

BMP-30 Infantry Fighting Vehicle

Bulgaria developed the BMP-30 from the Russian BMP-2

The BMP-30 was developed from the BMP-23 – which has a two man turret armed with a 23mm cannon, 7.62mm co-axial machine gun and Sagger ATGM (Anti-Tank Guided Missile) launcher – and has the same turret as that fitted to the Russian BMP-2 ICV.

The two man power-operated turret is armed with a 30mm rapid fire cannon and 7.62mm co-axial machine gun. Mounted on the turret roof is a launcher for the AT-4 Spigot with a range of 2000 m or AT-5 Spandrel with a range of 4,000m ATGM (Anti-Tank Guided Missile). The layout of the BMP-

30 is unusual, with the driver front right and powerpack to his rear, and one infantrymen at the front, on the left. The turret is in the centre, with the troop compartment at the rear with two roof hatches and twin doors at the rear.

The vehicle is fully amphibious, propelled in the water by its tracks at a maximum speed of 4.5km/h. Standard equipment includes firing ports/vision devices, a fire detection and suppression system, an NBC (Nuclear, Biological, Chemical) system and night vision equipment. It can also lay its own smoke screen by injecting diesel fuel into the exhaust outlet on the right side of the hull.

Specification

Crew: 2 + 11
Armament:
Main: 1 x 30mm cannon
Co-axial: 1 x 7.62mm machine gun
ATGM (Anti-Tank Guided Missile): 1 x Spandrel
Combat weight: 15,000kg (33,000lb)
Power-to-weight ratio: 20hp/t
Hull length: 7.127m (23.4ft)
Width: 2.85m (9.3ft)

Height: 2.115m (7ft)
Ground clearance: 0.40m (1.3ft)
Maximum road speed: 61.5km/h (38.1mph)
Range: 600km (372 miles)
Vertical obstacle: 0.80m (2.6ft)
Trench: 2.5m (8.2ft)
Fording: amphibious
Powerpack: YaMZ-238N diesel developing 302hp coupled to manual transmission

NORINCO YW 531 H APC

Chinese forces have a family of vehicles based on the YW531

The YW 531 H armoured personnel carrier is very similar to the YW 534 and is the successor to the older YW 531. More recently, the YW 531 H has been renamed by the Chinese as the Type 85 family of vehicles.

  The hull of the YW 531 H is an all-welded steel armour construction with the engine on the right side, driver front left, with commander to his rear and troop compartment extending to the rear. The latter is provided with roof hatches, a door extending to the rear and firing ports/vision devices. The main armament comprises a roof-mounted 12.7mm machine gun that is provided with a shield. The YW 531 H is fully amphibious, propelled in the water by its tracks at a maximum speed of 6km/h. Standard equipment includes night vision equipment and an NBC (Nuclear, Biological, Chemical) system.

Other Chinese APC families include the Type 90 (tracked), the WZ 501 (based on Russian BMP-1), the Type 77 and the WZ 551 (6 x 6).

Variants

YW 309 infantry combat vehicle (turret similar to Russian BMP-1)
WZ 751 armoured ambulance with raised roof
Type 85 armoured command post
NVH-1 mechanised infantry combat vehicle
Type 85 recovery vehicle
Type 85 maintenance engineering vehicle
Type 85 82mm mortar
122mm self-propelled gun

Specification

Crew: 2 + 13
Armament: 1 x 12.7mm machine gun
Combat weight: 13,600kg (28,600lb)
Power-to-weight ratio: 23.5hp/t
Hull length: 6.125m (20 1ft)
Width: 3.06m (10ft)
Height: 2.586m (8.5ft)

Ground clearance: 0.46m (1.5ft)
Maximum road speed: 65km/h (40mph)
Range: 500km (310 miles)
Vertical obstacle: 0.60m (2ft)
Trench: 2.20m (7.2ft)
Fording: amphibious
Powerpack: BF8L413F V-8 diesel, developing 320hp coupled manual transmission

NORINCO YW 531C APC

Many Iraqi YW 531s were captured during the Gulf War

The YW 531 was the first full tracked armoured personnel carrier to enter service with the Chinese Army and is also referred to as the K-63. Early production models were powered by the Type 6150L diesel engine. This vehicle was used in large numbers by Iraq in the 1991 Middle East conflict.

The late production model is the YW 531C which has a number of improvements including a different engine, a shield for the 12.7mm machine gun, new vision ports and improved ventilation. The hull of the YW 531 is an all-welded steel armour construction, with the engine on the right side and the troop compartment at the rear. The latter is provided with roof hatches, a door in the rear and firing ports/vision devices.

The YW 531 is fully amphibious, propelled in the water by its tracks at a maximum speed of 6km/h. Standard equipment includes night vision equipment and a roof-mounted 12.7mm machine gun. Standard production vehicles do not have a an NBC (Nuclear, Biological, Chemical) system, but a ventilation system is fitted as standard.

Variants
Anti-tank vehicle with four missiles
YW 304 82mm mortar
YW 381 120mm mortar
YW 701 command post vehicle
YW 750 ambulance
122mm self-propelled gun
130mm rocket launcher (Type 70)

Specification

Crew: 2 + 13
Armament: 1 x 12.7mm machine gun
Combat weight: 12,600kg (27,720lb)
Power-to-weight ratio: 25.39hp/t
Hull length: 5.476m (17.9ft)
Width: 2.978m (9.8ft)
Height: 2.58m (8.5ft)

Ground clearance: 0.45m (1.5ft)
Maximum road speed: 65km/h (40.3mph)
Range: 500km (310 miles)
Vertical Obstacle: 0.60m (2ft)
Trench: 2.00m (6.6ft)
Fording: amphibious
Powerpack: BF8L413F V-8 diesel developing 320hp coupled to manual transmission

OT-64C(1) APC

Polish and Czech forces continue to operate the OT-64 series

The OT-64 family of 8 x 8 armoured personnel carriers was jointly developed by the former Czechoslovakia and Poland, and used by them in place of the Russian equivalent, the BTR-60 series. The vehicle entered service in 1964, and production continued until 1990.

   In many respects the OT-64 is a better design than that of the Russian BTR-60 series, as the former has twin doors at the rear for the rapid entry/exit of troops. The final production model, the OT-64C(1), or SKOT-2A, as it is referred to, has the same one man manually operated turret as is fitted to the Russian BRDM-2 (4 x 4) reconnaissance vehicle and the BTR-60PB (8 x 8) armoured personnel carrier. Some models have a Sagger ATGM (Anti-Tank Guided Missile) launcher on either side of the turret.

All members of the family are fully amphibious, propelled in the water at a speed of 9km/h by two propellers mounted at the rear of the hull. Standard equipment includes an NBC (Nuclear, Biological, Chemical) system and night vision equipment, as well as power steering on the front four wheels, a winch and a central tyre pressure regulation system.

Variants
DPT-65 repair
OT-64 R series (command and radio)

Specification

Crew: 2 + 15
Armament:
Main: 1 x 14.5mm machine gun
Co-axial: 1 x 7.62mm machine gun
Combat weight: 14,500kg (31,900lb)
Power-to-weight ratio: 12.41hp/t
Hull length: 7.44m (24.4ft)
Width: 2.55m (8.4ft)
Height: 2.71m (8.9ft)

Ground clearance: 0.46m (1.5ft)
Maximum road speed: 94.4km/h (58.5ft)
Range: 710km (441 miles)
Vertical obstacle: 0.5m (1.6ft)
Trench: 2m (1.24ft)
Fording: amphibious
Powerpack: Tatra 928-18 V-8 diesel, developing 180hp coupled to semi-automatic transmission.

Kader Fahd APC

Developed from a German APC, the Fahd is in full production

In the 1980s the German company of Thyssen Henschel developed a 4 x 4 armoured personnel carrier, the TH 390, for the German Army. Production of this was then undertaken by the Kader Factory For Developed Industries, with first production vehicles of the so-called Fahd being completed in 1986. It is estimated that, by 1995, over 500 vehicles had been built for home and export markets.

To reduce procurement and life cycle costs, the Fahd is based on a Mercedes-Benz LAP 1117/32 truck chassis, fitted with a fully armoured body which provides the occupants with protection from small arms fire and shell splinters. The basic vehicle can carry ten troops, plus its two man crew, but a wide range of optional extras are available including a front-mounted winch, a central tyre pressure regulation system, passive night vision equipment, an air conditioning system, an NBC (Nuclear, Biological, Chemical) system and grenade launchers.

Various armament installations can also be fitted including 7.62mm and 12.7mm turret-mounted machine guns, a 20mm cannon and the complete turret of the BMP-2 infantry combat vehicle, which is armed with a 30mm cannon, 7.62mm co-axial machine gun and a roof-mounted ATGM (Anti-Tank Guided Missile). This is known as the Fahd 30.

Specification

Crew: 2 + 10
Armament: see text
Combat weight: 10,900kg (23,980lb)
Power-to-weight ratio: 15.4hp/t
Hull length: 6m (19.7ft)
Width: 2.45m (8ft)
Height: 2.1m (6.9ft)
Ground clearance: 0.31/0.37m (1ft/1.2ft)

Maximum road speed: 90km/h (55.8mph)
Range: 800km (496 miles)
Vertical obstacle: 0.7m (2.3ft)
Trench: 0.9m (2.95ft)
Fording: 0.7m (2.3ft)
Powerpack: Mercedes-Benz OM 352A 6-cylinder diesel developing 168hp coupled to manual transmission

Giat AMX-10P Infantry Fighting Vehicle

The amphibious AMX-10P is armed with a 20 mm cannon

The AMX-10P was developed for the French Army, with the first prototypes completed in 1968 and production carried out at the Giat Industries facility at Roanne, with first production vehicles completed in 1973.

The standard AMX-10P is fitted with a two man power operated turret armed with a 20mm cannon with a 7.62mm machine gun mounted co-axially. The vehicle is fully amphibious, propelled by water-jets at a maximum speed of 7km/h.

Standard equipment includes an NBC (Nuclear, Biological, Chemical) system, crew compartment heater and passive night vision equipment.

Listed below is a resume of some production variants, with the AMX-10 PAC 90 Marine having the TS 90 two man turret armed with a 90mm gun, used by Indonesia and Singapore. It weighs 14,800 kg and carries seven men – a crew of three and four infantrymen.

Variants
Ambulance
Anti-tank (HOT anti-tank guided missile)
Fire support
Command Marine

Specification

Crew: 3 + 8
Armament:
Main: 1 x 20mm cannon
Co-axial: 1 x 7.62mm machine gun
Combat weight: 14,500kg (31,900lb)
Power-to-weight ratio: 20.68hp/t
Hull length: 5.778m (19ft)
Width: 2.78m (9.1ft)
Height: 2.57m (8.4ft)

Ground clearance: 0.45m (1.5ft)
Maximum road speed: 65km/h (40.3mph)
Range: 600km (372 miles)
Vertical obstacle: 0.7m (2.3ft)
Trench: 2.1m (6.9ft)
Fording: amphibious
Powerpack: Hispano-Suiza HS 115 V-8 diesel, developing 300hp coupled to pre-selective transmission.

Giat AMX VCI Infantry Fighting Vehicle

The VCI is based on the chassis of the AMX-13 light tank

After the end of the Second World War, France developed the AMX-13 light tank and the chassis of this vehicle was then used for a completed family of other vehicles including the AMX VCI infantry combat vehicle. First AMX VCI prototypes were completed in 1955, with first production vehicles following in 1957. Production was originally undertaken at Roanne by the now Giat Industries, but was later transferred to Mecanique Creusot-Loire, which was subsequently taken over by Giat Industies. In French Army service the AMX VCI has almost been replaced by the AMX-10P infantry combat vehicle.

Standard production vehicles were powered by a Sofam Model 8Gxb 8-cylinder petrol engine, developing 250hp coupled to a manual transmission, but more recently the vehicle has been marketed with the Detroit Diesel engine which has been fitted to modernised vehicles for the export market. In addition to a one man Giat turret armed with a 20mm cannon, a wide range of other armament options were offered including turret and pintle-mounted 7.62mm and 12.7mm machine guns.

Variants
Ambulance
Artillery support vehicle
Cargo
Command post
Fire control vehicle

Specification
Crew: 3 + 10
Armament:
Main: 1 x 20mm cannon
Combat weight: 15,000kg (33,000lb)
Power-to-weight ratio: 16.67hp/t
Hull length: 5.7m (18.7ft)
Width: 2.67m (8.8ft)
Height: 2.41m (8ft)
Ground clearance: 0.48m

(1.6ft)
Maximum road speed: 64km/h (40mph)
Range: 500km (310 miles)
Vertical obstacle: 0.65m (2.1ft)
Trench: 1.6m (5.2ft)
Fording: 1m (3.3ft)
Powerpack: Detroit Diesel Model 6V-53T, developing 280hp coupled to manual transmission

Giat VAB Armoured Personnel Carrier

Over 5000 VABs have been built in many different versions

The VAB family of 4 x 4 and 6 x 6 armoured personnel carriers was developed for the French Army from 1970, with first prototypes completed in 1972. First production vehicles were completed in 1976 and, by 1995, over 5,000 had been built for the home and export markets.

In French Army service, the VAB is normally fitted with a 7.62mm or 12.7mm machine gun, but for the export market a wide variety of armament installations are offered including anti-tank guided weapons and surface-to-air missiles. The VAB is fully amphibious, propelled in the water by its wheels, but optional water-jets can be fitted to increase its water speed to 7km/h. Further development has resulted in a 'new generation' VAB with many improvements including greater protection, a more powerful engine, automatic transmission and an optional central tyre pressure regulation system.

Variants
Ambulance
Anti-aircraft (gun)
Anti-aircraft (missile)
Anti-tank (MILAN)
Anti-tank (HOT)
Artillery fire control
Command post

Specification (6 x 6)

Crew: 2 + 10
Armament: 1 x 12.7mm machine gun
Combat weight: 14,200kg (31,311lb)
Power-to-weight ratio: 15.49hp/t
Hull length: 5.98m (19.6ft)
Width: 2.49m (8.2ft)
Height: 2.06m (6.8ft)
Ground clearance: 0.4m (1.3ft)
Maximum road speed: 92km/h (57mph)
Range: 1000km (620 miles)
Vertical obstacle: 0.5m (1.6ft)
Trench: 1.0m (3.3ft)
Fording: amphibious
Powerpack: Renault MIDS 06-20-45 6-cylinder diesel, developing 220bhp coupled to Transfluide transmission

177

Panhard VCR APC

Some VCRs had been sold to Iraq before the 1991 Gulf War

The Panhard VCR (6 x 6) armoured personnel carrier was developed as a private venture from 1975 with the prototypes shown in 1977. It shares many common components with the Panhard ERC Sagaie (6 x 6) armoured car, developed at the same time.

The vehicle can be fitted with a wide range of armament installations, for example a turret armed with a 20mm cannon or 7.62mm/12.7mm machine guns at the front and a rail-mounted 7.62mm machine gun at the rear. The basic APC is called the VCT/TT.

Fully amphibious, the vehicle is propelled in the

water by its wheels at a maximum speed of 4km/h. Steering is power assisted on the front wheels, and the center wheels can be raised while travelling on roads. In addition to the wide range of turret options, the vehicle can also be fitted with an NBC (Nuclear, Biological, Chemical) system, various night observation devices, land navigation system, an air conditioning system and a front-mounted winch with a capacity of 3,000kg.

Variants
AT repair vehicle
AA anti-aircraft vehicle
TH anti-tank vehicle with HOT ATGM (Anti-Tank Guided Missile)

Specification

Crew: 3 + 9
Armament: 1 x 20mm cannon
Combat weight: 7,900kg (17,420lb)
Power-to-weight ratio: 18.35hp/t
Hull length: 4.875m (16ft)
Width: 2.50m (8.2ft)
Height: 2.26m (7.4ft)
Ground clearance: 0.315m (1.2ft)

Maximum road speed: 90km/h (56mph)
Range: 700km (434 miles)
Vertical obstacle: 0.8m (2.6ft)
Trench: 1.1m (3.6ft)
Fording: amphibious
Powerpack: Peugeot V-6 petrol, developing 145hp coupled manual transmission.

Panhard M3 APC

More than 20 different armies now operate the M3 APC

The M3 (4 x 4) armoured personnel carrier was developed by Panhard as a private venture, with the first prototype being completed in 1969 and first production vehicles following in 1971. The M3 shares many common components with the Panhard AML (4 x 4) armoured car.

The M3 is fully amphibious, propelled in the water by its wheels and, in addition to the wide range of armament options available, it can also be fitted with an NBC (Nuclear, Biological, Chemical) system, an air conditioning system, passive night vision devices and smoke grenade launchers.

The M3 can be fitted with various armament

options, with a typical fit being a turret armed with twin 7.62mm machine guns at the front, behind the driver, and a 7.62mm machine gun on a rail mount at the rear. Heavier turrets, for example armed with a 20mm cannon can also be fitted. The latest production version is the Buffalo, and has a number of improvements.

Variants
VDA 2 x 20mm self-propelled anti-aircraft gun
VAT repair
VPC command
VLA engineer
VTS ambulance
M3 radar

Specification

Crew: 2 + 10
Armament: see text
Combat weight: 6,100kg (20,000lb)
Power-to-weight ratio: 14.75hp/t
Hull length: 4.45m (14.6ft)
Width: 2.4m (7.9ft)
Height: 2.48m (8.1ft)
Ground clearance: 0.35m (1.1ft)

Maximum road speed: 90km/h (55.8ft)
Range: 600km (372 miles)
Vertical obstacle: 0.3m (0.9ft)
Trench: 0.8m (2.1ft)
Fording: amphibious
Powerpack: Panhard Model 4 HD 4-cylinder petrol, developing 90hp coupled to manual transmission.

Thyssen Henschel Marder 1A3

The Marder was one of the first infantry combat vehicles

The Marder 1 infantry combat vehicle was developed for the German Army from the late 1950s, with production being undertaken from 1970 to 1975 by the now Thyssen Henschel and MaK companies.

Since it first entered service, it has been constantly upgraded, with the latest version known as the Marder 1A3, and featuring additional hull and turret armour, as well as rearranged roof hatches, upgraded suspension, a new heating system and revised stowage. The two man power operated turret is armed with the same 20mm Rheinmetall cannon as is fitted to the Spahpanzer Luchs armoured reconnaissance vehicle (8 x 8) used by the German Army, with a 7.62mm machine gun being mounted co-axially. The 20mm cannon is not stabilised. Some vehicles have a MILAN

ATGM (Anti-Tank Guided Missile) system mounted on the turret. The Marder 1 is not amphibious, although with preparation it can ford to a depth of 2m.

Standard equipment includes an NBC (Nuclear, Biological, Chemical) system, a crew compartment heater and passive night vision equipment.

The Argentinian TAM medium tank is armed with a 105mm gun, and its associated VCTP infantry combat vehicles are based on the Marder chassis. Production of these has been completed and they are only used by Argentina.

Variants
Radar Roland 2 SAM

Specification

Crew: 3 + 6
Armament:
Main: 1 x 20mm cannon
Co-axial: 1 x 7.62mm machine gun
Combat weight: 35,000kg (77,000lb)
Power-to-weight ratio: 18hp/t
Hull length: 6.88m (22.6ft)
Width: 3.38m (11.1ft)
Height: 3.015m (9.9ft)
Ground clearance: 0.455m (1.5ft)
Maximum road speed: 65km/h (40.3mph)
Range: 500km (310 miles)
Vertical obstacle: 1.0m (3.3ft)
Trench: 2.5m (8.2ft)
Fording: 1.5m (5ft)
Powerpack: MTU MB 833 Ea-500 6-cylinder diesel, developing 600hp coupled to automatic transmission

Thyssen Henschel Transportpanzer 1

The Fuchs is now back in production for the export market

The Transportpanzer 1 (Fuchs) armoured personnel carrier was developed in the late 1960s, with production being carried out by the now Thyssen Henschel company.

The original German Army order was for 996 vehicles, which were delivered between 1970 and 1986. Since then, the Transportpanzer 1 vehicle has been placed back in production for the export market, with a number of countries placing orders for the NBC (Nuclear, Biological, Chemical) reconnaissance vehicle, used during the 1991 Gulf conflict, and which has the US Army designation of the M93 Nuclear, Biological and Chemical Reconnaissance System.

The vehicle is fully amphibious, propelled in the water by two propellers mounted at the rear of the hull, giving the vehicle a maximum water speed of 10.5km/h.

Standard equipment includes an NBC (Nuclear, Biological, Chemical) system, as well as power steering on the front four wheels, run flat tyres and passive night vision equipment. German Army vehicles are normally fitted with a roof-mounted 7.62mm machine gun.

For the export market a wide range of Variants are offered including repair, recovery, mortar carrier, anti-tank and internal security.

Specification

Crew: 2 + 10
Armament: 1 x 20mm cannon or 1 x 7.62mm machine gun
Combat weight: 17,000kg (37,400lb)
Power-to-weight ratio: 18.82hp/t
Hull length: 6.83m (22.4ft)
Width: 2.98m (9.8ft)
Height: 2.30m (7.5ft)
Ground clearance: 0.406m (1.3ft)

Maximum road speed: 105km/h (65.1mph)
Range: 800km (496 miles)
Vertical obstacle: 0.60m (2ft)
Trench: 1.10m (3.6ft)
Fording: amphibious
Powerpack: Mercedes-Benz OM 402A V-8 diesel, developing 320hp coupled to automatic transmission

185

Thyssen Henschel Condor APC

A Condor fitted with turret-mounted 20mm cannon

The Condor (4 x 4) armoured personnel carrier was developed as a private venture by Thyssen Henschel, with the first prototype completed in 1978. To reduce procurement and life cycle costs, proven and in-service automotive components are used wherever possible. The largest order for the Condor was placed by Malaysia, which ordered a total 459 in a number of versions, including ones fitted with a one man turret armed with 20mm cannon and 7.62mm co-axial machine gun, a one man turret armed with twin 7.62mm machine guns, a command post vehicle and a fitter's vehicle.

The Condor is fully amphibious, propelled in the water by an optional propeller mounted at the rear of the hull, giving a maximum water speed of 10km/h.

Standard equipment includes run flat tyres and power steering. A wide range of turrets can also be fitted on the roof of the Condor, as can pintle-mounted 7.62mm or 12.7mm machine guns. Optional equipment includes an air conditioning system, night vision devices, an NBC (Nuclear, Biological, Chemical) system and a winch with 50m of cable.

Variants
Ambulance
Anti-tank (missile)
Command post

Specification

Crew: 2 + 12

Armament:
Main: 1 x 20mm cannon
Co-axial: 1 x 7.62mm machine gun

Combat weight: 12,400kg (27,280lb)

Power-to-weight ratio: 13.54hp/t

Hull length: 6.13m (20.1ft)
Width: 2.47m (8.1ft)
Height: 2.79m (9.2ft)

Ground clearance: 0.475m (1.6ft)

Maximum road speed: 100km/h (62mph)

Range: 900km (558 miles)

Vertical obstacle: 0.55m (1.8ft)

Trench: nil

Fording: amphibious

Powerpack: Daimler-Benz OM 352A 6-cylinder diesel, developing 168hp coupled to manual transmission

Thyssen TM 170 APC

A TM 170 with its obstacle-clearing blade lowered

The TM 170 (4 x 4) armoured personnel carrier was developed by Thyssen Maschinenbau as a private venture and, like the earlier UR-416, is based on the chassis of the Mercedes-Benz UNIMOG (4 x 4) cross-country chassis. By 1995, over 250 had been built for the home and export markets. The German Border Guard and State Police version is known as the SW4.

The hull is an all-welded steel armour construction, with the powerpack, commander and driver at the front and the troop compartment extending to the rear. In addition to the doors in the side of the hull, there is also a ramp in the hull rear. Various weapon mounts can be fitted onto the roof including remote controlled 7.62mm machine gun, a turret armed with twin 7.62mm machine guns, a turret with 20mm cannon and various types of ATGM (Anti-Tank Guided Missile) such as Euromissile MILAN.

Standard equipment includes bullet-proof windows, while optional equipment includes propellers for amphibious operations, an obstacle clearing blade at the front of the hull, electrically operated smoke grenade dischargers, an auxiliary heater, a fire detection and suppression system, a winch, a public address system, an NBC (Nuclear, Biological, Chemical) system and run flat tyres.

Specification

Crew: 2 + 10
Armament: 1 x 7.62mm machine gun
Combat weight: 11 200kg (24 640lb)
Power-to-weight ratio: 15hp/t
Hull length: 6.14m (20.1ft)
Width: 2.47m (8.1ft)
Height: 2.32m (7.6ft)
Ground clearance: 0.48m (1.6ft)

Maximum road speed: 100km/h (62mph)
Range: 870km (539.4miles)
Vertical obstacle: 0.6m (2ft)
Trench: n/ap
Fording: 1.2m (4ft)
Powerpack: Daimler-Benz OM-352 turbo-charged diesel, developing 168hp coupled to manual transmission

PSZH-IV APC

PSZHs serve with former Warsaw Pact armies and Iraq

Further development of the Hungarian FUG (4 x 4) amphibious scout car resulted in the PSZH-IV (4 x 4) armoured personnel carrier which has also been referred to as the PSZH D-944.

The commander and driver are seated at the front of the vehicle, with the troop compartment in the center and the powerpack at the rear. The one man turret is armed with a 14.5mm machine gun, with a 7.62mm machine gun mounted co-axially. The driver and commander are each provided with a roof-hatch, and there is also a door in either side of the hull.

Unlike the Russian BRDM-1 and BRDM-2 (4 x 4) vehicles, the PSZH-IV does not have any belly wheels that are lowered to improve the cross-country mobility of the vehicle.

Standard equipment includes power assisted steering, NBC (Nuclear, Biological, Chemical) system and a central tyre pressure regulation system that allows the driver to adjust the tyre pressure to suit the terrain being crossed. It also has night vision equipment. The PSZH-IV is fully amphibious, propelled in the water by two water-jets mounted at the rear of the hull.

Variants
Ambulance
NBC (Nuclear, Biological, Chemical) reconnaissance
Command post

Specification

Crew: 3 + 6
Armament:
Main: 1 x 14.5mm machine gun
Co-axial: 1 x 7.62mm machine gun
Combat weight: 7,600kg (16,720lb)
Power-to-weight ratio: 13.15hp/t
Hull length: 5.695m (18.7ft)
Width: 2.50m (8.2ft)
Height: 2.308m (7.6ft)

Ground clearance: 0.42m (1.4ft)
Maximum road speed: 80km/h (50mph)
Range: 500km (310 miles)
Vertical obstacle: 0.40m (1.3ft)
Trench: 0.6m (2ft)
Fording: amphibious
Powerpack: Csepel D.414.44 4-cylinder diesel. developing 100hp coupled to manual transmission.

FIAT – OTO Melara Type 6614 APC

The Type 6614 is armed with a single 12.7 mm machine gun

The Type 6614 (4 x 4) armoured personnel carrier was developed as a private venture by FIAT (now IVECO) and OTO Melara (now OTOBREDA), with the former responsible for the hull and automotive aspects, and the latter for the turret and weapon system. The first prototype was completed in 1972, with first production vehicles completed shortly afterwards. The Type 6614 armoured personnel carrier car shares many common automotive components with the Type 6616, also developed by FIAT and OTO Melara.

Mounted on top of the roof is a one man manually operated cupola, with a single piece hatch cover, five periscopes and an externally mounted 12.7mm machine gun. The vehicle is fully amphibious, propelled in the water by its wheels at a maximum speed of 5km/h.

Standard equipment includes a power operated ramp at the rear, firing ports and associated vision devices, powered steering, run flat tyres and electric bilge pumps. As built, it was not fitted with passsive night vision equipment, smoke grenade dischargers, a fire detection and suppression system, an NBC (Nuclear, Biological, Chemical) system or a winch.

Variants
Mortar carrier

Specification

Crew: 1 + 10
Armament: 1 x 12.7mm machine gun
Combat weight: 8,500kg (18,700lb)
Power-to-weight ratio: 18.82hp/t
Hull length: 5.86m (19.2ft)
Width: 2.50m (8.2ft)
Height: 2.18m (7.2ft)
Ground clearance: 0.485m (1.6ft)

Maximum road speed: 100km/h (62mph)
Range: 700km (434 miles)
Vertical obstacle: 0.4m (0.2ft)
Trench: nil
Fording: amphibious
Powerpack: FIAT model 8062.24 super-charged diesel. developing 160hp coupled to manual transmission

Mitsubishi Type 73 APC

The Type 73 has a bow-mounted 7.62 mm machine gun

The Type 73 armoured personnel carrier was
developed from the late 1960s, and 225 vehicles were
built for the Japanese Ground Self Defence Force by
the time production was completed in 1989.

An unusual feature of the Type 73 and the earlier
Type SU 60 is that they both have a bow-mounted
7.62mm machine gun which can be traversed 30
degrees to the left or right, up or down. The bow
machine gunner is seated at the front of the hull, on
the left, with the driver to the right. The commander
is seated behind the driver, with the engine
compartment to the rear of the bow machine gunner.
Main armament comprises a 12.7mm machine gun
which can be aimed and fired from within the

vehicle. The troop compartment is at the rear of the hull and has roof hatches and twin doors. As built, the Type 73 is not amphibious, but when fitted with a kit, the vehicle is amphibious, propelled in the water by its tracks at a speed of 7km/h.

Standard equipment includes T-type firing ports in the sides and rear of the hull, an NBC (Nuclear, Biological, Chemical) system and night vision equipment.

Variants
Command vehicle
Ground wind measuring system
Mine clearing system

Specification

Crew: 3 + 9
Armament:
Main: 1 x 12.7mm machine gun
Bow: 1 x 7.62mm machine gun
Combat weight: 13,300kg (29,260lb)
Power-to-weight ratio: 22.6hp/t
Hull length: 5.8m (19ft)
Width: 2.8m (9.2ft)
Height: 2.2m (7.2ft)

Ground clearance: 0.40m (1.3ft)
Maximum road speed: 70km/h (43.4mph)
Range: 300km (186 miles)
Vertical obstacle: 0.70m (2.3ft)
Trench: 2m (13.1ft)
Fording: amphibious
Powerpack: Mitsubishi 4ZF V4 diesel, developing 300hp coupled to manual transmission.

BMP-3 Infantry Fighting Vehicle

The BMP-3 has been exported to Kuwait and the UAE

The BMP-3 was developed in the late 1980s as the replacement for the BMP-2 infantry combat vehicle and first seen in public in 1990.

The two man power operated turret is armed with a 100mm rifled gun which, in addition to firing high explosive fragmentation rounds at a rate of fire of eight to ten rounds a minute, can also fire a laser beam riding missile out to a maximum range of 4000m. A 30mm cannon is mounted co-axially to the right of the 100mm gun, with a 7.62mm machine gun mounted co-axially to the left. In addition, there are two bow-mounted 7.62mm machine guns. The vehicle is fully amphibious, propelled in the water to a maximum speed of 10km/h by two water-jets mounted at the rear of the hull.

Standard equipment includes firing ports/vision devices, a fire detection and suppression system, an NBC (Nuclear, Biological, Chemical) system, and night vision equipment. It can also lay its own smoke screen by injecting diesel fuel into the exhaust outlet on the right side of the hull. A dozer blade is carried retracted under the front of the vehicle.

Variants
BMP-3 reconnaissance vehicle
BMP-3 with thermal sight

Specification

Crew: 3 + 7
Armament:
Main: 1 x 100mm gun
Co-axial: 1 x 30mm cannon
Co-axial: 1 x 7.62mm machine gun
Bow: 2 x 7.62mm machine gun
Combat weight: 18,700kg (41,140lb)
Power-to-weight ratio: 26.73hp/t
Hull length: 7.20m (23.6ft)
Width: 3.23m (10.6ft)
Height: 2.65m (8.7ft)

Ground clearance: 0.45m (1.476ft)
Maximum road speed: 70km/h (43.4mph)
Range: 600km (372 miles)
Vertical obstacle: 0.80m (2.624ft)
Trench: 2.2m (23.7ft)
Fording: amphibious
Powerpack: Type UTD-29M 10-cylinder diesel, developing 500hp coupled to hydro-mechanical transmission

BMP-2 Infantry Fighting Vehicle

BMP-2s are in widespread service with ex-Soviet allies

The BMP-2 was developed in the late 1970s as the replacement for the BMP-1 infantry fighting vehicle, and was first seen in public in 1982. It is a further development of the BMP-1, with the most significant improvements being additional armour protection and the installation of a new two man power operated turret armed with a 30 mm rapid fire cannon and 7.62mm co-axial machine gun. Mounted on the turret roof is a launcher for the AT-4 Spigot or AT-5 Spandrel ATGM (Anti-Tank Guided Missile) system.

The vehicle is fully amphibious, propelled in the water by its tracks at a maximum speed of 7km/h.

Standard equipment includes firing ports/vision devices, a fire detection and suppression system, an NBC (Nuclear, Biological, Chemical) system and night vision equipment. It can also lay its own smoke screen by injecting diesel fuel into the exhaust outlet on the right side of the hull. Late production vehicles have additional armour protection for the hull and turret.

Production of the BMP-2 was undertaken in Czechoslovakia under the designation BVP-2, and it s currently being built, as the Sarath, in India, where many variants of it have been developed.

Variants
BMP-2K command vehicle
Mine clearing vehicle

Specification

Crew: 3 + 7
Armament:
Main: 1 x 30mm cannon
Co-axial: 1 x 7.62mm machine gun
Anti-tank: 1 x Spandrel ATGM (Anti-Tank Guided Missile)
Combat weight: 14,300kg (31,460lb)
Power-to-weight ratio: 20.30hp/t
Hull length: 6.735m (22.1ft)
Width: 3.15m (10.3ft)

Height: 2.45m (8.1ft)
Ground clearance: 0.42m (1.4ft)
Maximum road speed: 65km/h (40.3mph)
Range: 600km (372 miles)
Vertical obstacle: 0.70m (2.3ft)
Trench: 2.5m (8.2ft)
Fording: amphibious
Powerpack: Type UTD-20 6-cylinder diesel, developing 300hp coupled to manual transmission

BMP-1 Infantry Fighting Vehicle

The BMP-1 was the first true infantry combat vehicle

The BMP-1 infantry fighting vehicle was developed in the early 1960s and was first seen in public in 1967. Since then, it has been built in large numbers for the home and export markets. Further development has resulted in the improved BMP-2.

In the Russian Army the BMP-1 was the replacement for the BTR-50 full tracked APC and, compared to this vehicle, has a significant increase in armour, mobility and firepower. The BMP-1 has a one man turret armed with a 73mm gun fed by an automatic loader with a 7.62mm coaxial machine gun and a launch rail for a Sagger ATGM (Anti-Tank Guided Missile) over the 73mm gun. The vehicle is fully amphibious, propelled in the water by its tracks at a maximum speed of 7 km/h.

Standard equipment includes firing ports/vision devices, a fire detection and suppression system, an NBC (Nuclear, Biological, Chemical) system and night vision equipment. It can also lay its own smoke screen by injecting diesel fuel into the exhaust outlet on the right side of the hull.

Variants
BMP-1K command vehicle
BRM/BRM-1/BRM-1K reconnassance
PRP-3/PRP-4 radar
Mine-clearing vehicle

Specification

Crew: 3 + 8
Armament:
Main: 1 x 73mm gun
Co-axial: 1 x 7.62mm machine gun
Anti-tank: 1 x Sagger ATGM (Anti-Tank Guided Missile)
Combat weight: 13,500kg (29,700lb)
Power-to-weight ratio: 22.22hp/t
Hull length: 6.74m (22.1ft)
Width: 2.94m (9.6ft)

Height: 2.15m (7.1ft)
Ground clearance: 0.39m (1.3ft)
Maximum road speed: 65km/h (40.3mph)
Range: 600km (372 miles)
Vertical obstacle: 0.80m (2.6ft)
Trench: 2.2m (7.2ft)
Fording: amphibious
Powerpack: Type UTD-206-cylinder diesel, developing 300hp coupled to manual transmission.

BMD-1 Airborne Combat Vehicle

BMDs have seen action in Afghanistan and Somalia

The BMD-1 was developed for Russian air assault divisions and entered service in 1970.

The BMD-1 has the complete turret of the BMP-1 infantry combat vehicle and is armed with a 73mm gun fed by automatic loader with a 7.62mm coaxial machine gun and a launch rail for a Sagger ATGM (Anti-Tank Guided Missile) over the 73mm gun. There are also two bow-mounted 7.62mm machine guns. An unusual feature of the BMD-1 is its hydro-pneumatic suspension, allowing the driver to adjust ground clearance from 0.1 to 0.45m. The vehicle is fully amphibious, propelled by two water-jets at the rear of the hull at a maximum speed of 10km/h.

Standard equipment includes firing ports/vision devices, a fire detection and suppression system, an

NBC (Nuclear, Biological, Chemical) system as well
as night vision equipment. It can also lay its own
smoke screen by injecting diesel fuel into the exhaust
outlet on the right side of the hull.

Variants
BMP-1P
82mm mortar
BTR-D APC
IV118 artillery observation vehicle
1V119 artillery fire direction centre vehicle
BRehM-D repair vehicle 2S9 120mm mortar
Carrying Shmel-1 RPV

Specification

Crew: 3 + 4
Armament:
Main: 1 x 73mm gun
Co-axial: 1 x 7.62mm machine
gun
Bow: 2 x 7.62mm machine gun
Anti-tank: 1 x Sagger ATGM
(Anti-Tank Guided Missile)
Combat weight: 7,500kg
(16,500lb)
Power-to-weight ratio: 32hp/t
Hull length: 5.4m (17.7ft)
Width: 2.63m (8.6ft)

Height: 1.62/1.97m (5.3/6.4ft)
Ground clearance: 0.45m
(1.5ft)
Maximum road speed:
70km/h (43.4mph)
Range: 320km (198 miles)
Vertical obstacle: 0.80m (2.6ft)
Trench: 1.6m (5.2ft)
Fording: amphibious
Powerpack: Type 5D-20 6-
cylinder diesel, developing
240hp coupled to manual
transmission

BTR-80 APC

The BTR-80 was the third development of the BTR-60

The BTR-80 (8 x 8) armoured personnel carrier was developed as the replacement for the older BTR-70 (8 x 8) vehicle which is very similar in appearance with first production vehicles being completed in 1984.

Main improvements include replacement of the two petrol engines by a single diesel engine, a turret mounted machine guns to increase elevation, a bank of six smoke grenade launchers mounted on the turret rear, and providing the infantry with improved firing ports and vision devices. Entry and exit for the crew between the second and third road wheels has also been made easier. Over the frontal arc armour protection has also been improved. The BTR-80 is fully amphibious, propelled in the water by a single water-jet mounted at the rear of the hull. Before entering the water, the trim vane is erected at the front of the vehicle and the bilge pumps switched on.

Standard equipment includes a manually operated turret armed with one 14.5mm and one 7.62mm machine gun, central tyre pressure regulation system, an NBC (Nuclear, Biological, Chemical) system and night vision devices for commander, driver and gunner.

Variants
BTR-80A
Command post vehicle
120 mm 2S23 self-propelled gun
RKhM-4 chemical reconnaissance vehicle
Various civilian versions

Specification

Crew: 3 + 7
Armament:
Main: 1 x 14.5mm machine gun
Co-axial: 1 x 7.62mm machine gun
Combat weight: 13,600kg (29,920lb)
Power-to-weight ratio: 15.44hp/t
Hull length: 7.65m (25.1ft)
Width: 2.90m (9.5ft)

Height: 2.35m (7.8ft)
Ground clearance: 0.475m (1.6ft)
Maximum road speed: 80km/h (50mph)
Range: 600km (372 miles)
Vertical obstacle: 0.5m (1.6ft)
Trench: 2m (6.7ft)
Fording: amphibious
Powerpack: V-8 diesel, developed 210hp coupled to manual transmission.

BTR-70 APC

The BTR-70 introduced more powerful 8-cylinder engines

The BTR-70 (8 x 8) armoured personnel carrier was developed in the late 1970s as the replacement for the older BTR-60 (8 x 8) vehicle and was seen in public for the first time in 1980.

It is similar in appearance to the late production BTR-60PB, but has a number of improvements including larger tyres, more powerful engines and small door in the lower hull-side between the second and third road wheels. The BTR-70 is fully amphibious, propelled in the water at a maximum speed of 10km/h by a single water-jet mounted at the rear of the hull. Before entering the water, the trim vane is erected at the front of the vehicle and the bilge pumps are switched on.

Standard equipment includes a manually operated

turret armed with one 14.5mm and one 7.62mm machine gun, a central tyre pressure regulation system, power steering on the front four wheels, a front mounted winch, an NBC (Nuclear, Biological, Chemical) system and night vision devices for commander, driver and gunner.

Variants

BTR-70 with BTR-80 turret
BTR-70kh chemical reconnaissance vehicle
BTR-70MS communications
BTR-70KSSShM command post
BREM repair and recovery vehicle SPR-2 jammer

Specification

Crew: 2 + 9
Armament:
Main: 1 x 14.5mm machine gun
Co-axial: 1 x 7.62mm machine gun
Combat weight: 11,500kg (25,300lb)
Power-to-weight ratio: 20.86hp/t
Hull length: 7.535m 24.7ft)
Width: 2.80m (9.2ft)
Height: 2.235m (7.3ft)

Ground clearance: 0.475m (1.6ft)
Maximum road speed: 80km/h (49.6mph)
Range: 600km (372miles)
Vertical obstacle: 0.5m (1.6ft)
Trench: 2.0m (6.6ft)
Fording: amphibious
Powerpack: 2 x ZMZ-4905 8-cylinder petrol, developing 120hp each, coupled to two manual transmissions

BTR-60PB APC

Over 30 armies are equipped with the BTR-60 series

The BTR-60 (8 x 8) armoured personnel carrier was developed in the late 1950s as the replacement for the older BTR-152 (6 x 6) vehicle and was seen in public for the first time in 1961. The first version was the BTR-60P with an open roof, followed by the BTR-60PA (or BTR-60PK), with a fully enclosed troop compartment and, finally, the BTR-60PB, with a turret.

The BTR-60 is fully amphibious, propelled in the water at a maximum speed of 10 km/h by a single water-jet mounted at the rear of the hull. Before entering the water, the trim vane is erected at the front of the vehicle and the bilge pumps are switched on.

Standard equipment on BTR-60PB includes a manually operated turret armed with one 14.5mm and a 7.62mm machine gun, a central tyre pressure regulation system, as well as power steering on the front four wheels, a front-mounted winch, an NBC (Nuclear, Biological, Chemical) system and night vision devices for commander, driver and gunner.

Variants
BTR-60P
BTR-60PA
BTR-60PB
BTR-60PBK command
Number of other command, communication and observation vehicles

Specification

Crew: 2 + 14
Armament:
Main: 1 x 14.5mm machine gun
Co-axial: 1 x 7.62mm machine gun
Combat weight: 10,300kg (22,660lb)
Power-to-weight ratio: 17.47hp/t
Hull length: 7.56m (24.8ft)
Width: 2.825m (9.3ft)
Height: 2.31m (7.6ft)

Ground clearance: 0.475m (1.6ft)
Maximum road speed: 80km/h (49.6mph)
Range: 500km (310 miles)
Vertical obstacle: 0.4m (1.3ft)
Trench: 2m (6.6ft)
Fording: amphibious
Powerpack: 2 x GAZ-49B 6-cylinder petrol engines, developing 90hp coupled to manual transmission

MT-LB Multi-Purpose Tracked Vehicle

An MT-LB multi-purpose vehicle towing an anti-tank gun

The MT-LB armoured multi-purpose tracked vehicle was developed in the late 1960s to undertake a wide range of battlefield roles, including use as an armoured personnel carrier and towing artillery weapons such as the 122mm D-30 howitzer and 100mm T-12 anti-tank gun. The MT-LB is fully amphibious, propelled in the water by its tracks at a maximum speed of 4.5km/h. Before entering the water, a trim vane is erected at the front of the vehicle and the bilge pumps are switched on.

Standard equipment includes a turret-mounted 7.62mm machine gun, an NBC (Nuclear, Biological, Chemical) system and night vision devices. For operations in snow and swampy terrain it can also be fitted with wider tracks to reduce ground pressure and improve traction. The vehicle has also been made under licence in Bulgaria and Poland.

Variants
MT-LBV APC
MT-LBU command
MT-LB with SNAR-10 radar
MTP-LB repair vehicle
MT-LB ambulance
MT-LB engineer vehicle
RKhM chemical reconnaissance vehicle
MT-LB with Vasilek mortar
MT-LB with AT-6 ATGM (Anti-Tank Guided Missile)
MT-LB with 120mm mortar
SA-13 SAM system

Specification

Crew: 2 + 11
Armament: 1 x 7.62mm machine gun
Combat weight: 11,900kg (26,180lb)
Power-to-weight ratio: 20.16hp/t
Hull length: 6.454m (21.2ft)
Width: 2.86m (9.4ft)
Height: 1.865m (6.1ft)
Ground clearance: 0.4m (1.3ft)

Maximum road speed: 61.5km/h (38.1mph)
Range: 500km (310 miles)
Vertical obstacle: 0.61m (2ft)
Trench: 2.41m (8ft)
Fording: amphibious
Powerpack: YaMZ 238 V-8 diesel developing 240hp coupled to manual tranmission, with 6 forward gears and 1 reverse gear.

213

Reumech Sandock Ratel FSV 90

South African Ratels have seen action in Angola

The Ratel family of 6 x 6 armoured vehicles was developed by Sandock-Austral (now Reumech Sandock) for the South African Army. The first prototype was completed in 1974, with production running from 1978 through to 1987.

The driver is at the front, the turret is in the centre with a power-operated door either side, a powerpack left rear and passage way on the right rear. There is also a door in the rear on the right side. The Ratel Fire Support Vehicle 90 has a two man turret armed with a 90mm gun, 7.62mm co-axial machine gun and 7.62mm anti-aircraft machine gun, with an additional 7.62mm machine gun mounted at the right rear. The Ratel 20 infantry fighting vehicle has a two man turret armed with 20mm cannon, 7.62mm co-axial machine gun and two 7.62mm anti-aircraft machine guns.

Variants

Ratel 60
Ratel 12.7mm command
Ratel armoured repair vehicle
Ratel 81mm mortar carrier
Ratel tank destroyer, (Anti-Tank Guided Missile)
Ratel artillery observation vehicle

Specification

Crew: 3 + 7
Armament:
Main: 1 x 90mm gun
Co-axial: 1 x 7.62mm machine gun
Anti-aircraft: 2 x 7.62mm machine gun
Combat weight: 19,000kg (41,800lb)
Power-to-weight ratio: 14.84hp/t
Hull length: 7.212m (23.7ft)
Width: 2.516m (8.3ft)

Height: 2.915m (9.6ft)
Ground clearance: 0.34m (1.1ft)
Maximum road speed: 105km/h (97.7mph)
Range: 1000km (620 miles)
Vertical obstacle: 0.6m (2ft)
Trench: 1.15m (3.8ft)
Fording: 1.2m (3.9ft)
Powerpack: D 3256 BTXF 6-cylinder turbo-charged diesel, developing 282hp coupled to automatic transmission.

TFM Casspir APC

The Casspir APC was used during the war in Namibia

The first Casspir mine protected vehicles were based on a Bedford (4 x 4) truck chassis, but the Mk II and Mk III were developed by the TFM company from the early 1980s for South Africa. The latest vehicle is the Casspir Mk III and, like the ealier vehicles, has a special all-welded steel hull which provides a high degree of protection from mines. If the vehicle does run over an anti-tank mine, the wheel would be blown off, while the occupants survive. The engine is at the front, with the commander and driver to its rear; the troop compartment extends to the rear, where two entry doors are provided. Bullet-proof windows and firing ports are standard.

Standard equipment also includes two spare wheels and a drink water tank, while optional equipment includes a pneumatically controlled drop-down front bumper for clearing obstacles. There is no NBC (Nuclear, Biological, Chemical) system.

Variants
Ambulance
Artillery fire control
Command post vehicle
Internal security
Mine detection vehicle
Mine clearance vehicle
Tanker (Duiker)
Recovery vehicle (Gemsbok)

Specification

Crew: 2 + 10
Armament: 1 or 3 x 7.62mm machine gun
Combat weight: 12,580kg (27,676lb)
Power-to-weight ratio: 13.51hp/t
Hull length: 6.87m (22.5ft)
Width: 2.50m (8.2ft)
Height: 2.85m (9.3ft)
Ground clearance: 0.41m (1.3ft)
Maximum road speed: 90km/h (55.8mph)
Range: 850km (527 miles)
Vertical obstacle: 0.50m (1.64ft)
Trench: 1.06m (3.5ft)
Trench: 1.06m (3.5ft)
Powerpack: ADE-352T 6-cylinder diesel, developing 170hp coupled to manual transmission

Reumech Sandock Mamba Mk II APC

South Africa is now exporting the distinctive Mamba Mk II

The Mamba Mk II (4 x 4) armoured personnel carrier is a further development of the Mamba Mk I (4 x 2) as developed by Mechem Consultants. By early 1995 Reumech Sandock had built over 500, with Alvis of the UK also having a licence.

The Mamba Mk II has a hull of all-welded steel armour construction, designed to provide the occupants with the maximum possible protection should the vehicle run over a mine. The powerpack is at the front, the commander and driver in the centre, and the troop compartment at the rear. The troops are seated four down either side, facing each other. They enter and leave via a large door in the rear. There are a total of eight hatches in the roof.

Standard equipment includes bullet-proof windows all round, with the option of firing ports, as well as power steering and a 100 litre water tank. The standard Mamba Mk II has a wheel base of 2.9m, but a version with a wheelbase of 2.38m is also available.

Variants

Ambulance
Command post
Logistic support
Recovery
Utility vehicle

Specification

Crew: 2 + 9
Armament: 1 x 7.62mm machine gun
Combat weight: 6,800kg (14,960lb)
Power-to-weight ratio: 18.08hp/t
Hull length: 5.46m (18ft)
Width: 2.205m (7.2ft)
Height: 2.495m (8.2ft)

Ground clearance: 0.39m (3ft)
Maximum road speed: 102km/h (63.3mph)
Range: 900km (558 miles)
Vertical obstacle: 0.41m (1.4ft)
Trench: 0.90m (3ft)
Fording: 1m (3.3ft)
Powerpack: Daimler-Benz OM 352 6-cylinder diesel, developing 123hp at 2800rpm

Santa Barbara BLR APC

The BLR is offered with manual or automatic transmission

The BLR (4 x 4) armoured personnel carrier was developed by Pegaso for the Spanish Marines and Police, with production and marketing now being carried out by SBB Blindados SA, part of the Santa Barbara Group.

The basic vehicle is fitted with a Santa Barbara one man cupola with eight vision blocks and an externally mounted 7.62mm machine gun, with a shield provided for the gunner. Powerpack options include a diesel engine coupled to a manual transmission, and a diesel engine coupled to a fully automatic transmission.

Standard equipment includes power-assisted steering, a ventilating system and a semi-automatic fire suppression system. Channels can be carried to enable the vehicle to cross trenches and other obstacles.

A wide range of other optional equipment has also been offered for the BLR including front mounted obstacle clearing blade, CS gas dischargers activated by the vehicle commander, as well as load speakers, sirens, a power take-off, run flat tyres, a front-mounted winch with a capacity of 4,500kg, night vision equipment and various types of communications equipment. Other armament installations include turret mounted weapons such as 20/25mm cannon and 90mm guns.

Specification

Crew: 1 + 12
Armament: 1 x 7.62mm machine gun
Combat weight: 12,000kg (26,400lb)
Power-to-weight ratio: 17.5hp/t
Hull length: 5.65m (18.5ft)
Width: 2.5m (8.2ft)
Height: 2m (6.6ft)
Ground clearance: 0.32m (1ft)

Maximum road speed: 93km/h (57.7mph)
Range: 570km (353 miles)
Vertical obstacle: 0.4m (1.3ft)
Trench: n/a
Fording: 1.1m (3.6ft)
Powerpack: Pegaso 6-cylinder diesel, developing 210hp coupled to ZF manual transmission

Santa Barbara BMR-600 APC

The BMR-600 is armed with a 12.7 mm machine gun

The BMR-600 (6 x 6) armoured personnel carrier was developed by Pegaso for the Spanish Army, with the first prototype completed in 1975 and first production vehicles in 1979. Production and marketing is now carried out by Santa Barbara and total production has now reached over 1,500 vehicles for the home and export markets.

The BMR-600 shares many common automotive components with the VEC cavalry scout vehicle (6 x 6), although this has a different layout. The standard production BMR-600 is fitted with a 12.7mm M2 machine gun which can be aimed and fired from within the cupola. The BMR-600 is fully amphibious, propelled in the water by its wheels although, as an option, two water-jets can be mounted on either side of the hull rear.

Standard equipment includes hydro-pneumatic suspension, steering on the front and rear wheels, NBC (Nuclear, Biological, Chemical) system, night vision equipment and a winch.

Variants
Ambulance
Command post vehicle
Engineer vehicle
Radio communications vehicle
Recovery and maintenance vehicle
81mm or 120mm mortar carrier
90mm gun vehicle

Specification

Crew: 2 + 11
Armament: 1 x 12.7mm machine gun
Combat weight: 14,000kg (30,800lb)
Power-to-weight ratio: 22hp/t
Hull length: 6.15m (20.17ft)
Width: 2.5m (8.2ft)
Height: 2.36m (7.7ft)
Ground clearance: 0.4m (1.3ft)

Maximum road speed: 103km/h (63.9mph)
Range: 1,000km (620 miles)
Vertical obstacle: 0.6m (0.4ft)
Trench: 1.5m (4.9ft)
Fording: amphibious
Powerpack: Pegaso 9157/8 6-cylinder diesel, developing 310hp coupled to ZF 6 HP 500 automatic transmission.

9040 Infantry Combat Vehicle

The CV 9040 series is in service with Sweden and Norway

The Combat Vehicle 9040 infantry fighting vehicle was developed for the Swedish Army, with Hagglunds Vehicle being responsible for the chassis, and Bofors for the two man power operated turret and 40mm cannon. Following extensive trials, the CV 9040 was adopted by the Swedish Army, with the first of an estimated 600 production vehicles being completed in 1993.

The 40mm L/70 cannon has been developed from the famous 40mm L/70 anti-aircraft gun. Turret traverse and weapon elevation are powered, but the 40mm cannon is not stabilised. The basic CV 9040 has day/night observation equipment for commander, gunner and driver, an NBC (Nuclear, Biological, Chemical) system and a heater. It is not amphibious.

To meet the requirements of the Norwegian Army, Hagglunds Vehicle developed the CV 9030 and, in 1995, an order was placed for 110 vehicles. CV 9030 has a different turret armed with a 30mm McDonnell Douglas Helicopters Chain Gun and a 7.62mm co-axial machine gun, with the main armament being stabilised.

Variants
CV 9025
CV 9030 or CV 9040 anti-aircraft
CV 90 forward command vehicle
CV 90 forward observation vehicle
CV 90 ARV (Armoured Recovery Vehicle)

Specification

Crew: 3 + 8
Armament:
Main: 1 x 40mm cannon
Co-axial: 1 x 7.62mm machine gun
Combat weight: 22,400kg (49,280lb)
Power-to-weight ratio: 24.55hp/t
Hull length: 6.471m (21.1ft)
Width: 3.01m (9.9ft)
Height: 2.50m (8.2ft)

Ground clearance: 0.49m (1.6ft)
Maximum road speed: 70km/h (43.4mph)
Range: 500km (310 miles)
Vertical obstacle: undisclosed
Trench: undisclosed
Fording: undisclosed
Powerpack: Scania DS 14 diesel, developing 550hp coupled to Perkins X-300-5 fully automatic transmission

Hagglunds Vehicle Pbv 302 APC

Pbv 302s have been deployed with Swedish units serving with the UN

The Pansarbandvagn 302 (Pbv 302) was developed by Hagglunds Vehicle for the Swedish Army with production being undertaken from 1966 to 1971.

The driver is seated at the front, in the centre, with the gunner to his left and the vehicle commander to the right. The troop compartment is at the rear of the hull and is provided with roof hatches and twin doors. The one man manually operated turret is armed with a 20mm cannon which can be elevated from -10 to +50 degrees, with the turret being capable of traverse a full 360 degrees.

The vehicle is fully amphibious, propelled in the water by its tracks at a maximum speed of 8km/h. Before entering the water, a trim vane is erected at the front of the hull and the bilge pumps are switched on. The vehicle is not fitted with an NBC (Nuclear, Biological, Chemical) system. For operating as part of United Nations forces in the former Yugoslavia, some Pbv 302 vehicles have been fitted with additional armour protection for improved battlefield survivability.

Other Hagglunds Vehicle AFVs include the Ikv-91 tank destroyer, the Brobv 941 bridgelayer and the Bgbv 82 armoured recovery vehicle.

Variants
Armoured command vehicle
Armoured observation post vehicle
Armoured fire direction post vehicle

Specification

Crew: 2 + 10
Armament: 1 x 20mm cannon
Combat weight: 13,500kg (29,700lb)
Power-to-weight ratio: 20.74hp/t
Hull length: 5.35m (17.5ft)
Width: 2.86m (9.4ft)
Height: 2.5m (8.2ft)
Ground clearance: 0.40m (1.3ft)

Maximum road speed: 66km/h (40.9mph)
Range: 300km (186 miles)
Vertical obstacle: 0.61m (1.2ft)
Trench: 1.8m (5.9ft)
Fording: amphibious
Powerpack: Volvo-Penta Model THD 100 B 6-cylinder diesel,developing 280hp coupled to manual transmission

MOWAG Piranha APC (LAV-25)

The US Marine Corps LAV-25 version of the Piranha

The Piranha family of 4 x 4, 6 x 6 and 8 x 8 family of vehicles was originally developed by MOWAG as a private venture and, as well as being made in Switzerland, has also been manufactured under licence in Canada (Diesel Division, General Motors), Chile (FAMAE) and the UK (GKN Defence).

All Piranha vehicles have a similar layout, with the driver front left, powerpack to his right and troop compartment at the rear. All of them have automotive components in common .

In the US Marine Corps the vehicle is known as the

Light Armored Vehicle (LAV), and uses the following 8 x 8 variants: the LAV-25mm cannon, LAV-R recovery and LAV-L logistics, the LAV-M 81mm mortar, as well as LAC-C command, LAV-AT anti-tank and LAV-EW electronic warfare. Canada has five different versions: the Bison (8 x 8) APC, the Cougar 76mm fire support (6 x 6), the Grizzly APC (6 x 6), the Husky recovery (6 x 6) and the LAV-25 reconnaissance (8 x 8). Saudi Arabia ordered 1117 in 10 versions: the LAV-25, the TOW anti-tank, the troop carrier, the 120mm mortar, the recovery, the command and control, the ambulance, the engineer and the assault gun and ammunition carrier.

Specification

Crew: 3 + 6
Armament:
Main: 1 x 25mm cannon
Co-axial: 1 x 7.62mm machine gun
Combat weight: 12,792kg (28,142lb)
Power-to-weight ratio: 21.49hp/t
Hull length: 6.393m (21ft)
Width: 2.449m (7.8ft)
Height: 2.692m (8.8ft)
Ground clearance: 0.392m (1.3ft)

Maximum road speed: 100km/h (62mph)
Range: 668km (414 miles)
Vertical obstacle: 0.50m (1.6ft)
Trench: 2.057m (6.7ft)
Fording: amphibious
Powerpack: Detroit Diesel Model 6V-53T 6-cylinder diesel, developing 275hp coupled to Allison fully automatic transmission

GKN Warrior Mechanised Combat Vehicle

The Desert version of the Warrior built for Kuwait

The Warrior mechanised combat vehicle was developed for the British Army. A total of 789 vehicles were delivered in seven versions between 1986 and 1995.

The standard Warrior section vehicle is fitted with a two man turret armed with a 30 mm RARDEN cannon and 7.62mm co-axial machine gun, with the turret in centre and troop compartment at the rear.

Standard equipment includes an NBC (Nuclear, Biological, Chemical) system and passive night vision equipment for commander, gunner and driver. For operation Desert Storm and operations in the former Yugoslavia, Warrior has been fitted with additional passive armour protection over the frontal arc.

In 1993, Kuwait placed an order for 254 Desert

Warrior vehicles and Variants. Desert Warrior has the US Systems Delco turret armed with a stabilised 25mm Chain Gun, a 7.62mm co-axial Chain Gun and a Hughes TOW ATGM (Anti-Tank Guided Missile) launcher mounted either side of the turret.

Variants
Warrior command
Warrior with MILAN Anti-Tank Guided Missile
Warrior mechanised recovery vehicle
Warrior mechanised combat repair vehicle
Warrior mechanised artillery observation vehicle
Warrior battery command vehicle
Desert Warrior

Specification

Crew: 3 + 7
Armament:
Main: 1 x 30mm cannon
Co-axial: 1 x 7.62mm machine gun
Combat weight: 25,700kg (56,540lb)
Power-to-weight ratio: 21.4hp/t
Hull length: 6.34m (70.2ft)
Width: 3.034m (10.8ft)
Ground clearance: 0.49m (1.6ft)

Maximum road speed: 75km/h (46.5mph)
Range: 660km (409.2miles)
Vertical obstacle: 0.75m (2.5ft)
Trench: 2.5m (8.2ft)
Fording: 1.3m (4.3ft)
Powerpack: Perkins Engines (Shrewsbury) Condor CV-8 TCA 8-cylinder diesel, developing 550hp to Perkins X-300-4B fully automatic transmission.

231

GKN Defence FV432 APC

FV432s are still used in for many roles by the British army

The FV432 series of full tracked APCs was developed for the British Army by the now GKN Defence. Over 3000 vehicles were built between 1963 and 1971. In the basic APC role it has been replaced by the Warrior mechanised combat vehicle, but it is still used for support roles by almost every arm of the British Army.

The standard FV432 has a one man manually operated turret armed with a 7.62mm machine gun, but these used in the support role are normally armed with a pintle-mounted 7.62mm machine gun. Passive night vision equipment is fitted as standard, as is an NBC (Nuclear, Biological, Chemical) system. The FV432 is very similar in appearance to the US United

Defense M113 series, which has a hull of all-welded aluminium armour and is fully amphibious. The FV432 has an all welded steel hull, but is not amphibious.

Variants
Ambulance
Command post vehicle
Artillery fire control vehicle
Mortar locating radar (Cymbeline)
81mm mortar vehicle
Maintenance vehicle
Engineer vehicle (inc minelaying)
Signals vehicle

Specification

Crew: 2 + 10
Armament: 1 x 7.62mm machine gun
Combat weight: 15,280kg (33,616lb)
Power-to-weight ratio: 15.7hp/t
Hull length: 5.251m (17.2ft)
Width: 2.8m (9.1ft)
Height: 2.286m (7.5ft)
Ground clearance: 0.406m (1.3ft)

Maximum road speed: 52.2km/h (32.3mph)
Range: 480km (298 miles)
Vertical obstacle: 0.609m (1.2ft)
Trench: 2.05m (6.2ft)
Fording: 1.066m (3.5ft)
Powerpack: Rolls-Royce K60 2-stroke 6-cylinder multi-fuel, developing 240hp coupled to TX-200-4A semi-automatic transmission.

GKN Defence Saxon APC

British Army Saxons have a pintle-mounted 7.62 mm machine gun

The Saxon (4 x 4) armoured personnel carrier was developed as a private venture and, wherever possible, uses standard commercial components. The first prototype was completed in 1975 and the first production models in 1976. By early 1995 well over 700 had been built.

The driver is seated at the front left or right, with the commander in the centre under the cupola, with the infantry on seats either side of the vehicle, facing inwards. Standard equipment includes power-assisted steering. Optional equipment includes firing ports/ vision devices, air conditioning, an auxiliary power unit, barricade remover, searchlight, heater, grenade launchers, loud speakers and run-flat tyres as well as a front-mounted winch. From 1990 it was offered with a Cummins 6BT turbo-charged diesel developing 160bhp coupled to an automatic transmission. Various weapons stations are available.

Variants
Ambulance
Command Post vehicle
Internal security
Patrol
Recovery Vehicle

Specification

Crew: 2+ 8
Armament: 1 x 7.62mm machine gun
Combat weight: 11,600kg (25,520lb)
Power-to-weight ratio: 14.06hp/t
Hull length: 5.169m (19.95ft)
Width: 2.489m (8.16ft)
Height: 2.626m (8.61ft)
Ground clearance: 0.41m

(1.34ft)
Maximum road speed: 96km/h (59.6mph)
Range: 480km (298 miles)
Vertical obstacle: 0.41m (1.34ft)
Fording: 1.12m (3.67m)
Powerpack: Bedford 500 6-cylinder diesel developing 164bhp coupled to automatic transmission

Alvis Saracen APC

Saracens serve with several Commonwealth forces

The Alvis Saracen (6 x 6) armoured personnel carrier was developed after the end of the Second World War, with the first prototypes built in 1952 and production carried out at Coventry between 1953 and 1972. The Saracen shares many common components with the Alvis Saladin (6 x 6) armoured car and the Stalwart (6 x 6) high mobility load carrier.

The engine is at the front. The driver to the immediate rear, and to his rear, on the left side, is the section commander. The radio operator is on the right. The troop compartment is at the rear, with the troops bseated facing each other. They enter and leave via two doors in the rear. The manually operated turret is armed with a 7.62mm machine gun and above the troop compartment at the rear is a Bren 7.62mm machine gun.

More recently, Alvis and A. F. Budge have developed a diesel upgrade package for the Saracen to extend its operational life into the 21st Century. Indonesia is the first customer for this upgrade package.

Variants
FV604 and FV610 command posts
FV611 ambulance

Specification

Crew: 2 + 10
Armament:
Main: 1 x 7.62mm machine gun
Anti-aircraft: 1 x 7.62mm machine gun
Combat weight: 10,170kg (22,374lb)
Power-to-weight ratio: 15.73hp/t
Hull length: 5.233m (17.2ft)
Width: 2.539m (8.3ft)
Height: 2.463m (8.1ft)

Ground clearance: 0.432m (1.4ft)
Maximum road speed: 72km/h (44.6mph)
Range: 400km (248 miles)
Vertical obstacle: 0.46m (1.5ft)
Trench: 1.52m (5ft)
Fording: 1.07m (3.5ft)
Powerpack: Rolls-Royce B80 petrol, developing 160hp coupled to preselector 5-speed transmission

Shorts S55 APC

Turkey, Malaysia and Pakistan are known users of the S55

Building on its experience in the design, development and production of the Shorland (4 x 4) armoured patrol car, Shorts went on to develop the Shorland armoured personnel carrier, with the first prototype completed in 1973 and the first production vehicle following in 1974. By early 1995, large numbers of Shorland armoured personnel carriers had been built and sales had been made to some 20 countries.

Since it first appeared, development has continued with the latest 5-series based on the Land Rover Defender 110 inch chassis, and having the option of a petrol or diesel engine. The basic S55 Shorland

238

armoured personnel carrier is unarmed, but provision is made for the installation of a 7.62mm machine gun on the roof, with the option of two banks of four electrically operated smoke grenade dischargers on either side of the hull. Standard equipment includes power steering, bullet-proof windows, extraction fans, an air conditioning system and seat belts. Optional equipment consists of drop-down visors with vision blocks in place of the bullet-resistant windscreen.

Variants
S52 armoured patrol car
S53 mobile air defence vehicle with SAMs
S54 anti-hijack vehicle

Specification

Crew: 3
Armament: 1 x 7.62mm machine gun
Combat weight: 3,600kg (7,920lb)
Power-to-weight ratio: 37.2bhp/t (petrol) 29.7bhp/t (diesel)
Hull length: 4.25m (13.9ft)
Width: 1.80m (5.9ft)
Height: 2.28m (7.4ft)
Ground clearance: 0.324m (1.06ft)
Maximum road speed: 120km/h (74mph)
Range: 630km (390 miles)
Vertical obstacle: 0.23m (0.8ft)
Trench: n/a
Fording: n/a
Powerpack: Rover 3.5 litre V8 petrol, developing 134bhp, or 2.5 litre Land Rover TDi diesel, developing 107bhp coupled to manual transmission.

239

United Defense M113A3 APC

The M901 version has TOW anti-tank missiles

The M113 series of armoured personnel carriers was developed by the FMC Corporation (now United Defense) for the US Army. First production vehicles were completed in 1960, with final deliveries being made in 1992. Since then, the production line has been reopened for Kuwait. Over 74,000 M113 series vehicles have been built, with licenced production also undertaken in Belgium and Italy.

The M113 vehicle had a petrol engine with the M113A1 being powered by a diesel engine. Later production models were the M113A2 and M113A3.

The M113 is fully amphibious, propelled in the water by its tracks at a maximum speed of 5.8km/h. Standard equipment includes an NBC (Nuclear, Biological, Chemical) system and passive night vision equipment.

Variants
M163 20mm self-propelled anti-aircraft gun
M577 command post
M730 Chaparral SAM
M901 Improved TOW Vehicle
Rapier SAM
Recovery
81mm, 107mm and 120mm mortar

Specification

Crew: 2 + 11
Armament: 1 x 12.7mm machine gun
Combat weight: 12,150kg (26,730lb)
Power-to-weight ratio: 22.29hp/t
Hull length: 5.30m (17.4ft)
Width: 2.686m (8.8ft)
Height: 2.54m (8.3ft)
Ground clearance: 0.43m (1.4ft)

Maximum road speed: 65.7km/h (40.7ft)
Range: 480km (298ft)
Vertical obstacle: 0.61m (2ft)
Trench: 1.68m (5.5ft)
Fording: amphibious
Powerpack: Detroit Diesel 6V-53T V-6 diesel, developing 275bhp coupled to Allison Transmission TX-200-4 automatic transmission.

AAV7A1 Amphibious Assault Vehicle

The US Marine Corps is the only operator of the huge AAV7 amphibian

The AAV7 amphibious assault vehicle was developed by the FMC Corporation, Ground Systems Division (now United Defense LP) as the replacement for the older LVTP5 series. First production vehicles were completed in 1971 and known as the Landing Vehicle, Tracked, Personnel, Model 7. The vehicle was subsequently known as the AAV7, with later production models being the AAV7A1. Production was completed in 1986.

The driver is at the front, on the left, with the commander to his rear and the powerpack on the right. The turret is to the rear of the powerpack, with the troop compartment extending to the rear, and provided with roof hatches and a power operated ramp. As built, it has a turret armed with a 12.7mm machine gun, but some US Marine Corps vehicles have the Upgunned Weapons Station with 40mm grenade launcher and 12.7mm machine gun plus additional armour protection. The vehicle is fully amphibious, propelled in the water at a maximum speed of 13.2km/h by two water-jets mounted at the rear of the hull.

Variants
AAVC7A1 command vehicle
AAVR7A1 recovery vehicle
AAV7A1 mine-clearing vehicle

Specification
Crew: 3 + 25
Armament: 1 x 12.7mm machine gun
Combat weight: 23,991kg (52,780lb)
Power-to-weight ratio: 16.67hp/t
Hull length: 7.943m (26.1ft)
Width: 3.27m (10.7ft)
Height: 3.263m (10.7)ft
Ground clearance: 0.406m (1.3ft)

Maximum road speed: 72.42km/h (45mph)
Range: 482km (1581 miles)
Vertical obstacle: 0.914m (3ft)
Trench: 2.438m (8ft)
Fording: amphibious
Powerpack: Cummins VT400 8-cylinder turbo-charged diesel, developing 400hp coupled to HS-400-3A1 automatic transmission

245

Cadillac Gage LAV-300 APC

A LAV-300 APC fitted with the 90 mm gun turret

The LAV-300 family of 6 x 6 armoured personnel carriers was developed as a private venture by Cadillac Gage Textron, now Textron Marine & Land Systems, based on their experience in the design, development and production of the LAV-150 series of 4 x 4 vehicles. The first prototypes were completed in 1979, with Panama and Kuwait being the first customers.

The layout of all vehicles is similar, with the driver front left and the powerpack to the right, the turret in centre and troop compartment at the rear. The LAV-300 is fully amphibious, propelled in the water by its wheels at a maximum speed of 4.8km/h.

Standard equipment includes firing ports/vision

devices, power steering and run-flat types. Optional equipment includes an NBC (Nuclear, Biological, Chemical) system and night vision devices.

Variants
Ambulance
Anti-tank with TOW Anti-Tank Guided Missile
Cargo carrier
Command post
81mm mortar
Various turrets fitted with 90mm gun, cannon or machine guns

Specification

Crew: 3 + 9
Armament:
Main: 1 x 20mm cannon
Co-axial: 1 x 7.62mm machine gun
Anti-aircraft: 1 x 7.62mm machine gun
Combat weight: 14,969kg (32,931lb)
Power-to-weight ratio: 18.94hp/t
Hull length: 6.40m (21ft)
Width: 2.54m (8.3ft)
Height: 2.692m (8.8ft)

Ground clearance: 0.533m (1.7ft)
Maximum road speed: 100km/h (62mph)
Range: 700km (434 miles)
Vertical obstacle: 0.609m (2ft)
Trench: 1.25m (4.1ft)
Fording: amphibious
Powerpack: Cummins 6 CTA 8.3 turbo-charged 6-cylinder diesel, developing 275hp coupled to 6-speed automatic transmission

247

Cadillac Gage LAV-150 APC

The LAV-150 can carry many different turrets, this has a 90mm gun

In 1962 the now Textron Marine & Land Systems, developed a 4 x 4 multi-role vehicle, the V-100 Commando. It was purchased by the US Army for use in Vietnam under the designation of the M706. The V-100 was followed by the larger V-200 only purchased by Singapore. The V-200 was followed by the improved V-150, then the V-150 S and, more recently, the V-150 ST (stretched and turbo-charged). In 1994 the V-150 family was renamed the LAV-150.

The LAV-150 is fully amphibious, propelled in the water by its wheels at a maximum speed of 5km/h.

Standard equipment includes firing ports/vision devices, power steering and run-flat types.

Variants

Anti-aircraft (20mm)
Anti-tank (TOW)
Command post
Internal security
81mm mortar
90mm gun and 7.62mm machine gun
25mm cannon and 7.62mm machine gun
20mm cannon and 7.62mm machine gun
12.7mm machine gun and 40mm grenade launcher
12.7mm and 7.62mm machine gun
Twin 7.62mm machine gun
Ring mount with 7.62mm machine gun

Specification

Crew: 3 + 2
Armament:
Main: 1 x 20mm cannon
Co-axial: 1 x 7.62mm machine gun
Anti-aircraft: 1 x 7.62mm machine gun
Combat weight: 9865.5kg (21,753.6lb)
Power-to-weight ratio: 42bhp/t
Hull length: 689m (18.6ft)
Width: 2.6m (7.4ft)

Height: 5.4m (8.3ft)
Ground clearance: 0.648m (2.1ft)
Maximum road speed: 87.8km/h (54.6 mph)
Range: 642km (399 miles)
Vertical obstacle: 0.9m (2 ft)
Trench: lm (3.28ft)
Fording: amphibious
Powerpack: 04 V-8 diesel, developing 202bhp coupled to 4-speed automatic transmission

Cadillac Gage Ranger APC

The Ranger is based on a standard Chrysler truck chassis

The Ranger (4 x 4) armoured personnel carrier was developed as a private venture by the former Cadillac Gage Textron company, now the Textron Marine & Land Systems Division of Textron Incorporated. The first prototype was completed in 1977, with first production vehicles following in 1980. The vehicle is not used by the US Army, but is used by the US Air Force and Navy for patrolling airfields, weapons storage sites and other high-risk areas.

The Ranger is essentially a modified Chrysler 4 x 4 truck chassis fitted with a welded steel armour body, which provides the occupants with protection from small arms fire and shell splinters. A variety of weapon fits can be mounted on the roof including an externally mounted 7.62mm machine gun, with a shield or a turret armed with either a twin 7.62mm machine gun or a combination of 7.62mm and 12.7mm machine guns. A wide range of optional equipment can be fitted including a siren/public address system, various radio installations, a spotlight, a grenade launcher system, a front-mounted winch and a 24-V electrical system.

Variants
Ambulance
Command post
Reconnaissance vehicle
VIP carrier

Specification

Crew: 2 + 6
Armament: 1 x 7.62mm machine gun
Combat weight: 4,536kg (9,979lb)
Power-to-weight ratio: 40hp/t
Hull length: 4.699m (15.4ft)
Width: 2.019m (6.6ft)
Height: 1.981m (6.5 ft)
Ground clearance: 0.203m (0.7ft)

Maximum road speed: 112km/h (69mph)
Range: 482km (299 miles)
Vertical obstacle: 0.254m (0.8ft)
Trench: n/a
Powerpack: Dodge 360 CID V-8 petrol, developing 180hp coupled to automatic transmission.

BVP M80A Infantry Fighting Vehicle

War in Yugoslavia stopped production of the M80A

The BVP M80A is a further development of the M-80 (which was previously called the M-980) and was shown for the first time in the early 1980s. It has been widely used in the recent civil war in Yugoslavia, but production has now stopped.

The driver and commander are seated behind each other at the front left with the powerpack to the right, one man turret in the centre and troop compartment at the rear. The latter is provided with roof hatches, twin doors at the rear and firing ports/vision devices. The twin launcher for the Sagger ATGM (Anti-Tank Guided Missile) is mounted on the turret roof at the rear. The vehicle is fully amphibious, propelled in the water by its tracks at a speed of 7.8km/h.

Standard equipment includes a fire detection and suppression system, an NBC (Nuclear, Biological, Chemical) system and night vision equipment. It can also lay its own smoke screen by injecting diesel fuel into the exhaust outlet on the right side of the hull.

Variants
Ambulance
Anti-aircraft (2 x 30mm or surface-to-air missile)
Anti-tank vehicle
Battaltion command post vehicle
Company command post vehicle
BVP M80AK with 30mm cannon

Specification

Crew: 3 + 7	**Height:** 2.67m (8.8ft)
Armament:	**Ground clearance:** 0.40m (1.3ft)
Main: 1 x 20mm cannon	
Co-axial: 1 x 7.62mm machine gun	**Maximum road speed:** 64km/h (38mph)
Anti-tank: 2 x Sagger ATGM (Anti-Tank Guided Missile)	**Range:** 500km (310miles)
Combat weight: 14,000kg (30,800lb)	**Vertical obstacle:** 0.80m (2.6ft)
	Trench: 2.4m (7.9ft)
Power-to-weight ratio: 22.5hp/t	**Fording:** amphibious
	Powerpack: FAMOS 10V003 10-cylinder diesel, developing 315hp coupled to manual transmission
Hull length: 6.42m (21.1ft)	
Width: 2.995m (9.8ft)	

Other titles in the Collins/Jane's Gems series will include:

Aircraft of World War II

A handy guide to the warplanes of World War II from the Battle of Britain to the airwar against Japan. Includes over 100 warplanes from all major air forces, with technical data and photographs. A historical introduction explains how the biplanes of the 1930s evolved into fast monoplane fighters and eventually jets.

Modern tanks

A complete guide to the tank forces of the 1990s, featuring over 100 combat vehicles with photographs and technical specifications. An introductory section reveals the latest developments in tank technology and explains how tanks are adapting to the new challenges of the modern battlefield. From veterans like the T-55 to the M1 Abrams and the XM-8, this includes every main battle tank produced since World War II.

Combat aircraft

A concise guide to military aircraft today, from the ultra-modern F-117 Nighthawk, better known as the 'Stealth' bomber to the veteran warplanes like the Boeing B-52 and McDonnell Douglas F-4 Phantom. An introductory section reveals the latest developments in military aircraft and how designs are changing now the Cold War is over.